THE HUNTINGTON BOTANICAL GARDENS

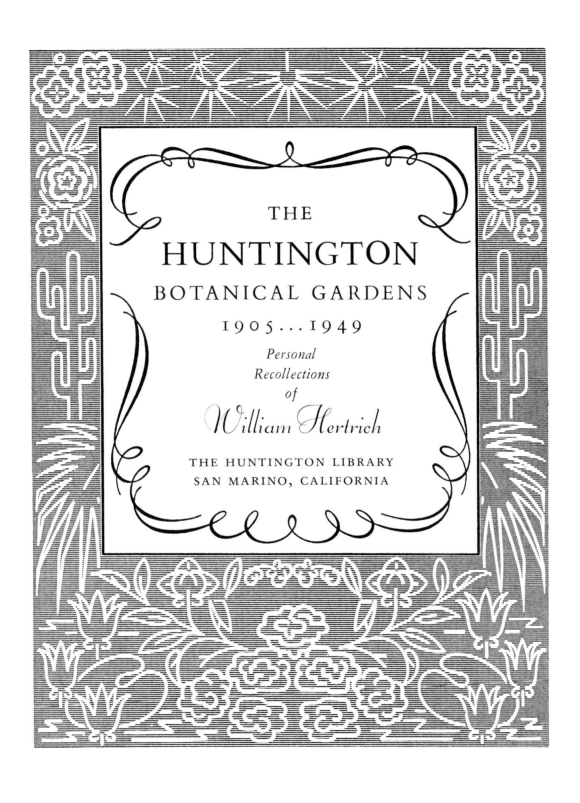

THE
HUNTINGTON
BOTANICAL GARDENS
1905...1949

Personal
Recollections
of

William Hertrich

THE HUNTINGTON LIBRARY
SAN MARINO, CALIFORNIA

Library of Congress Catalog Card No. 88-548
ISBN 0-87328-096-2

First edition, copyright 1949 by the
Henry E. Huntington Library and Art Gallery

Paperback reprint, with introduction by Myron Kimnach,
copyright 1988 by the
Henry E. Huntington Library and Art Gallery

Designed by Ray Smokel
Reprinted by The Castle Press, Pasadena, California

Contents

$\mathcal{F}$oreword

In 1962 I was surprised to receive a letter from William Hertrich, asking if I would be interested in applying for the position of Superintendent of Buildings and Grounds at the Henry E. Huntington Library and Art Gallery. I had, of course, heard of Mr. Hertrich but we had never met or corresponded. It seemed he had read some of my articles on plants and decided, with my experience at the University of California Botanical Garden, Berkeley, that I would be a good candidate for the job soon to be vacated by Howard Asper, who was leaving to carry on a nursery business.

I began my new job on November 1, at the end of the traditional October renovation of lawns and buildings. At that time the garden office, together with the institution's business office, occupied a small white building just east of the Library. My room had originally been Mr. Huntington's office, then had been occupied in turn by three superintendents, Mr. Hertrich, Ron Townsend, and Howard Asper.

On my first day I finally met Mr. Hertrich, who, since his retirement in 1948, had the use of a desk in the adjacent botanical library room. As I entered, he stood up, smiled and shook my hand in a most friendly manner. As usual, he was dressed formally in a suit and tie and held himself erect and with shoulders back; he thus always made a dignified appearance as he walked about the office or garden.

Until his death three years later in 1966, Mr. Hertrich came to the office several days a week. Because of his failing vision, his wife drove him through the grounds from their beautiful home on the north edge of the Huntington property. He took little interest in current garden projects, appearing to be immersed in the past. He was also very careful not to criticize my superintending; but once in a while he would gently point out some little oversight or problem he thought I should know about. I was grateful for his suggestions and glad to be let off so easily, as I had understood that when he retired he had been slow to loosen his grip on authority.

Mr. Hertrich's activities in those years I knew him were few but doubtless gratifying. Two years previously his eyesight had prevented him from completing the fourth volume of his work on camellias. But he could still look at photographs with a magnifying glass and he spent much time examining thousands of black-and-white prints of the gardens taken by him and others, partly to label but also, surely, to reminisce. Once he spent several days going over detailed, forty-year-old records of his fertilizing program for the orange groves, proudly showing me a drawing of an apparatus he had built to mix fertilizer with the irrigation water. He also went out for a long daily walk around the gardens; it must indeed have been satisfying to view the maturity of the many gardens he had designed and the size of the trees he had planted three to five decades earlier. There was always concern about his safety on these walks (particularly on the part of Margarete, his wife) due to his eyesight and the high summer temperatures, and one time he returned to his office bruised and bloody—he had a bad fall in the Desert Garden by stepping off a retaining wall. Yet everyone realized that these walks were necessary to his happiness. In 1966, aged 88, Mr. Hertrich suffered a stroke from which he never regained consciousness.

When he retired in 1948 at the age of 70, Mr. Hertrich found time to do much writing, completing books on palms and cycads, the Desert Garden, and three volumes on camellias. The first to be published (in 1949) was the present work in which he lovingly recalls his years at the Huntington. Some have found it an overly personal view, omitting, over-, or under-emphasizing the facts, but it was never intended as a formal history, as indicated by its subtitle: "Personal Recollections...." For a somewhat different account of the garden's formation, largely based on letters between Huntington and Hertrich, we can go to James Thorpe, "The Creation of the Gardens," in *The Founding of the Henry E. Huntington Library and Art Gallery: Four Essays* (1969).

For anyone interested in the Huntington or in the horticultural history of southern California, William Hertrich's book is a charming and absorbing account of the founding of a major research and cultural center and one of the world's great gardens. It well deserves this reprint edition.

MYRON KIMNACH

S A YOUNG LANDSCAPE GARDENER I SET OUT
early in 1903 from New England to visit my uncle who lived
on a ranch in Orange County, California. It was my desire
to make a success in the field of my profession.

I had devoted the previous ten years to the study and
practice of agriculture, horticulture, and landscape gardening.
This proved to be an excellent background; yet climatic differences between California and the countries from which
I had gained my experience necessitated a different application of principles which
could only be gained through practice. Since I had had an agricultural background,
citrus and walnut culture appealed to me as did later the growing of avocados, persimmons and other tropical or subtropical fruits.

In the fall of 1903 I accepted a position as landscape gardener to assist in planting
the L. K. Rindge Garden on Harvard Boulevard in Los Angeles. This and similar jobs
offered experience but did not appeal to me, for I desired a permanent position which
would definitely offer possibilities of future promotions and assure progress in my
chosen field.

In the spring of 1904 an attractive offer such as I had in mind opened up: it was
from a private estate in Connecticut. So, although still at work in California, I began
to make plans to return East to look over the situation and inspect the premises before
giving a definite answer. The day that I decided to buy my ticket, I stood in line for
an hour and then decided to have lunch and return for the ticket later. In a nearby
restaurant I shared a table with two other men; we discussed real estate values, among
other subjects of conversation, and also the recent extension of the streetcar lines and
building of new ones by H. E. Huntington, in the city and county of Los Angeles. We
all agreed that such expansion would inevitably attract capital and should therefore
bring large numbers of people from other parts of the country. It appeared evident to
all of us that Southern California enjoyed an almost unequalled opportunity to become
the winter resort of wealthy Easterners, some of whom undoubtedly would build
permanent homes in or near the metropolis. This conversation with its vision of the
future of Los Angeles caused me to cancel my plans for purchasing tickets to go East;
and soon thereafter I accepted a temporary position, deciding to bide my time until
an opening should come such as I desired.

A short time later I became acquainted with George J. Kuhrts, chief engineer of
the Los Angeles Railway Company, through whom I learned of Mr. Huntington's
intention to build a home in Southern California. George S. Patton was then general
manager of the Huntington Land and Improvement Company, and as such in charge

of all Huntington properties in Southern California, including San Marino Ranch. Mr. Kuhrts gave me a letter of introduction to Mr. Patton, who advised me that Mr. Huntington already had a landscape gardener. He asked me many questions, however, about my general background and experience, and before I left he indicated that he would contact me in the future, should such an opening as I was seeking become available. In December of that year, 1904, Mr. Patton offered me the position of landscape gardener of San Marino Ranch, subject to the approval of Mr. Huntington, who was then in New York.

As a bachelor I moved into the home of the former owner of the property, J. de Barth Shorb. The once magnificent mansion had greatly deteriorated because it had been vacant for some years. The two months following this move I spent in familiarizing myself with every section of the ranch property as I attempted to visualize possible landscape improvements. Thus it was that when Mr. Huntington returned for his winter visit in California, I was able to answer with some degree of certainty his questions regarding the development of his property. This proved of considerable benefit to me in our future relationships, since my new employer, though a man of wide vision and experience, was practical in every sense of the word.

Purchase of the Ranch

When Mr. Huntington became interested in choosing a homesite of his own in Southern California, several locations were considered; it first appeared that he might prefer the selection of city property when he purchased the former Childs estate, embracing the entire block between Eleventh and Twelfth Streets and from Main Street to Broadway. On this estate there was a pretentious home surrounded by a beautiful garden containing many exotic plants. Soon thereafter considerable property near Oneonta Junction in South Pasadena was acquired. About two blocks south of the Junction an elevated section of the property commanded a splendid view of the San Gabriel Valley to the south, and of the mountains to the north and east—an ideal location, it would seem, for a homesite. But in January 1903 Mr. Huntington became the owner of San Marino Ranch, and his preference for this among the three is easily understood.

When Mr. Huntington purchased the San Marino Ranch from the Farmers and Merchants Bank of Los Angeles as an investment, he believed, apparently, that it would some day become the site of his California home. He had known the place, as well as its former owner, since 1892 when he first visited Southern California and was the house guest of the Shorb family. Mr. Huntington never forgot his first impression as he gazed at the sunset from the south veranda of the Shorb home, overlooking the beautiful San Gabriel Valley.

To the north from San Marino Ranch was the view of the majestic Sierra Madre range of mountains, with Mount Wilson and Mount Lowe and "Old Baldy"; to the south was a beauteous, rolling countryside, much of it planted to citrus trees and to hay and grain; finally, as a backdrop, to the southeast extended the panoramic view of the Whittier hills. It was an almost unparalleled site on which structures of lasting beauty could be built to immense advantage, from the standpoint of architectural appreciation and aesthetic enjoyment, and so it remains today.

Plans for the gardens to surround the future Huntington residence necessarily had to be held in abeyance until Mr. Huntington should decide on the precise location of the home. He was very indefinite for a number of years, and in fact, it was not until he commissioned his architects, Myron Hunt and Elmer Grey, to prepare the plans, that the location was selected and the time of construction determined.

Improvements for the first two years were directed toward the laying out of an extensive drainage system to take care of excess storm water. In 1905 some of the border planting took place along San Marino Avenue from Huntington Drive to California Street, and westward in an irregular line to the Patton estate, following the west line to Huntington Drive and east to San Marino Avenue. A considerable portion of the ranch was located south of Huntington Drive. This was considered the commercial section and was planted to citrus and grain. In this section, also, was the packinghouse from which all the citrus fruit grown on the San Marino and El Molino ranches was shipped, as well as the fruit from the Patton and Bradbury ranches and from the orchards of Archie Smith, who managed the packinghouse.

Establishment of the Nursery

Realizing the great number of plants required to landscape this large estate, I suggested to Mr. Huntington that we start our own nursery to grow such material as was to be needed in tremendous quantities for mass plantings. I procured some seeds of redwood, and incense and Himalayan cedars, of Canary Island date and other palms, of pepper trees and numerous others. In a very few years we had growing in nursery rows and in the lath house over 15,000 plants. Many of these were later planted on the newly subdivided adjacent land to serve the purpose of street and lot improvements; and indeed, some of the redwoods, cedars, and oaks can still be seen in various parts of San Marino; for instance, the redwood in front of the City Hall, the palms on the Huntington School property, and the cedars along St. Albans and other streets, all originated as seedlings in that first little nursery.

Pepper trees were one of Mr. Huntington's favorites, and it was because of this that I made special efforts to grow a great number of them with as tall trunks as possible so that they might be planted effectively along Huntington Drive. It is considerable trouble to train these trees to grow ten-foot trunks to provide head clearance over streets and sidewalks, and to care for them for many years; but when they were planted they were greatly admired by everyone who saw them. When the widening of Huntington Drive was necessary, it was a great misfortune to have to eliminate all of these pepper trees, as well as about a thousand English laurel shrubs planted between them. Other trees have met a better fate by being planted within the boundaries of the Botanical Garden: at present there may be seen within these boundaries some of the tallest of the redwoods planted from seeds in 1905, some of them having attained heights ranging from seventy-five to one hundred feet. Along one of the drives inside the ranch more than a hundred Lebanon cedars were planted. The latter were imported from France as small plants.

Lily Ponds

Early in 1904 Mr. Huntington had engaged a landscape gardener recommended by a good friend of his. The appointment, unfortunately, was not satisfactory; but during the period of this particular man's employment, a small amount of border planting and the excavation for the lily ponds was done. Shortly after I arrived at the ranch we completed preparations for the ponds by putting in the concrete bottoms and walls. We then installed the connecting rockeries, built divisions and cement boxes to accommodate aquatic plants, and made ready to receive these plants. Most of the water lilies, lotus, and other aquatics were purchased from E. D. Sturdevant of Hollywood, a specialist in this category. The resulting ponds constituted the first complete unit of the gardens. A few years later important improvements effected other units.

I had hoped to grow tropical species of lilies, particularly the giant-leaved Amazon water lily, Victoria Regina, and I wanted to have the flowering season extended if possible into the winter months, that the Huntington family might enjoy them during winter sojourns. In order to bring this about I selected one of the large ponds and installed a thousand feet of two-inch galvanized pipe along the walls of the pond, then connected this to a hot-water boiler about four hundred feet away which was camouflaged by shrubbery. Distillate was used for fuel. This arrangement proved to be very satisfactory; thus, the flowering season of the tropical water lilies, including the giant-leaved Victoria, was extended to the middle of January.

The Water System

The former Shorb residence and the surrounding garden were supplied with water from a small triplex pump connected to two galvanized iron tanks installed in the tops of two towers, one adjacent to the residence, the other near the stable. They were not sufficient to meet new needs.

The water system inherited from the Shorb estate consisted of a large, open, dirt-bank reservoir with a capacity of about 4,000,000 gallons. It was supplied by nearby springs and wells. The reservoir was just high enough to irrigate the citrus orchards and alfalfa fields located below what is now known as Euston Road. To augment this supply of water Mr. Huntington acquired from George S. Patton, Ruth W. Patton and Annie Wilson on May 27, 1907, 65.81 acres of canyon property, including a water well of 100 miner's inches, drilled by A. K. Knudson in 1901, and all water rights to that area. About one fourth of this flowed without pumping during the winter months, thus taking care of the lower section.

In the upper section, however, it was obvious that before any extensive planting could be undertaken an additional water supply and reservoir storage had to be acquired. To meet this need a reservoir with a capacity of 100,000 gallons was built on the highest elevation of the ranch and connected with a well about one half mile to the south. This location is now the southwest corner of California Street and Hill Avenue. But this storage proved inadequate also for the job ahead, and another reservoir was subsequently built, located a half mile south and having a 2,000,000-gallon capacity. A ten-inch pipe line served as the distributive medium.

During Mr. Shorb's ownership of San Marino Ranch, he had sold water rights as follows: to Richard Garvey, February 29, 1892, 30 miner's inches of flowing water for distribution to a section five miles south of the ranch; and to a group of citrus growers, certain rights to the natural spring, without pumping privileges, at the mouth of Mission Canyon in the west section of the ranch.

[5]

The property involved in the transaction with the Garvey rights was located north of the original entrance drive to the Shorb estate along the eastern border line. It can be identified now only by stating that it occupied a position about five hundred feet north of the present Euston Road, and just east of Oxford Road. It was swampy land at the time, and when the swamp began to dry up it was found that highly valuable peat could be dug out of the ground. We hauled close to 8,000 wagon loads of this peat into the garden areas. It was especially helpful when we began the planting of a large area of *Lippia repens* to prevent erosion where we planned to establish a palm garden. Enriching the soil with the peat caused the *Lippia repens* to flourish quickly.

The purchasers of water rights had the additional privilege of sinking a well and pumping water not to exceed 30 miner's inches to be measured and checked through a weir trough. Mr. Huntington realized after purchasing the property that with the improvements he had planned such permanent water rights would be neither convenient nor agreeable. He offered to compensate the parties if they would cancel their rights, but they refused his offer. Nor did Mr. Huntington meet with any success when the case was brought to court.

The problem was solved, however, when the spring on the west side dried up and ceased flowing, due to the continuous lowering of the underground water-table. The rights to the 30 miner's inches were satisfactorily adjusted when the water company found that it would be obliged to replace the five-mile pipe line with a new one. But it was not until August 30, 1924, that Mr. Huntington acquired from the Garvey Water Company a deed to cover all rights, titles, and interest in possession of said company.

"Baching"

It was not very many months after I moved into the former Shorb residence, after taking up my new duties, that I became convinced that this solitary manner of living was tiresome. Although preferring quiet country life to the bustle of life in the city, it must be remembered that this was before the day of radio, telephone, gas, and electricity as items to be taken for granted. No such comforts were available and bachelor living had little attraction as a long-term prospect.

My mother was living at this time with my sister in Los Angeles, and she offered to come to keep house for me. Soon we were able to move into a small cottage that had been prepared for us in the midst of the orange orchard about 300 yards north of Huntington Drive. It proved to be a cozy enough little place and we loved the mode of living, although we had no neighbors and the nearest stores were in San Gabriel. Having the freedom of the ranch, however, I was entitled to any products grown or raised that were needed for the household. At that time I was earning $75 per month, and in addition to this I was allowed my cottage, plus the utilities available, as well as all necessary milk, poultry, and vegetable products. This was considered a very good wage in those days, when ranch labor was paid on the average of $1.25 per day and the highest pay was $1.50 for a nine-hour day.

Close to two years after coming to the ranch, in the fall of 1906, I married Margarete Stritzinger. We were married in the old mission at San Gabriel, after having driven there in an open carriage with a Mexican coachman. We settled in the same little cottage, and although there was lack of the conveniences we so take for granted now, which made our housekeeping comparatively primitive, we thoroughly enjoyed the next five years, living virtually in the midst of the orange groves. My good wife, Margarete, proved to be a most helpful assistant and a great comfort; I particularly needed her during those early years of strenuous work and endless responsibility. In 1910, Mr. Huntington built us a lovely modern bungalow on Huntington Drive, opposite Palmas Station, next to the two historic palms. Here we spent twenty of our very happy years together.

The two historical palms mentioned above are representatives of California's only native palm, the true desert Fan Palm (*Washingtonia filifera*), indigenous to the region around Palm Springs and found most frequently in canyons following a watercourse.

Rearing their lofty heads almost one hundred feet into the air, these two specimens are still in good condition. They have stood there during the entire development of the city of San Marino, and date still farther back: records reveal that they were planted there about 1840 by a prospector and miner, one of the earliest white settlers in this region. He apparently tried to duplicate their original environment in Palm Canyon, for he planted them near the stream of water coming from Mission Canyon to supply the needs of the San Gabriel Mission. It took days of laborious travel by burro to bring the trees to their present location, just north of Huntington Drive near Palmas station. In 1941 the San Marino Garden Club placed a bronze plaque on one of the trees as a step toward preserving them as historic landmarks.

The Palm Garden

Soon after taking up my work for Mr. Huntington, it became evident to me that he was particularly interested in the various types of cocos palms because of their tropical appearance as part of the landscape. I therefore suggested to him the establishment of a palm collection. In discussing the matter, we decided to introduce into Southern California palms from different parts of the world having similar climatic conditions; and we planned to test their suitability as landscape material for home gardens, parks, and street and highway plantings.

In 1905 we selected for this purpose four acres of sloping ground bordering on the main drive which was to lead to the proposed homesite. After grading, and installing a water system, the entire area was planted to *Lippia repens* as a ground cover to guard against erosion. It was about this time that the southern slopes to the west of the planned palm garden were similarly planted, and for the same reason: over 300,000 plants of the *Lippia repens* were used.

We soon found that collecting palms was a very slow process indeed. Some of the material I was then able to obtain locally, *i.e.,* in the counties of Los Angeles, Orange, San Diego, Ventura, and Santa Barbara. Rarer specimens I found in various horticultural establishments in the eastern states, and a few I obtained from nurseries in England, Belgium, and Germany. Some Asiatic species came from Japan.

As I went about collecting palms for outdoor planting, I looked also for tropical species to be used later in the proposed conservatory. Experiments in the open with more tropical species, even in sheltered places, proved only partially successful; most of them succumbed during the unusually cold years of 1913, 1922, and 1937. Our collection increased, however, during the years until we had accumulated about 450 specimens: these represented 148 species and varieties.

Orchard heating to a limited extent was practiced on the ranch, but, as stated elsewhere, it would have been impractical, under the existing circumstances, to extend this a great deal. During the winter of 1913 the temperature dropped to 20 degrees Fahrenheit, and we suffered a considerable loss of young plants. I shall never forget my initiation to the unpleasant task of smudging that January. Most of the orchard heaters were of the open-top type at that time. They were of two- or three-gallon capacity and, there was no doubt about it, they were capable of producing an abundance of smoke. Unfortunately I selected a block of navel oranges adjacent to the bungalow in which we lived. The bungalow had just been newly furnished with rugs, curtains, and drapes. I think my wife has never quite forgiven me for the damage done because of my choice of this section for experimenting with these 500 primitive heaters. Selection of that particular location was made because temperature readings during preceding years revealed it to be the coldest section of the citrus orchards anywhere on the ranch. Recorded readings showed the lowest temperatures to have been 27° and 28° previously but in 1913 the mercury went to a new low of 20°. The best we could do with these primitive heaters was to raise the temperature three degrees, insufficient to save the fruit but helping to keep the trees from severe damage.

By the time the second spell of severely cold weather occurred in 1922 we were much better prepared to protect the approximately twenty-five acres of citrus area, as we were equipped this time with modern heaters. By this time the navel orchard adjoining my home property fortunately had been abandoned and planted to alfalfa. About this time further improvement had been accomplished by the erection of a small reservoir for the storage of oil for the heaters; this was located at a spot which is now the southwest corner of the intersection of Oxford and Stratford Roads.

To emphasize the difficulties we encountered in trying to increase our tropical collections, the following weather data are pertinent: during the winter of 1913, as mentioned above, the low was 20° and we suffered considerable loss of young plants. In 1922, temperature records indicated 21°, 22°, and 23° Fahrenheit on three successive nights. This, too, resulted in additional loss of plants too tender to withstand such conditions: some plants suffered simply because they were immature. The most severe test came in January 1937. We experienced two separate cold periods approximately a week apart with a low temperature of 20° Fahrenheit. Fortunately, by then most of the plants previously endangered had reached a maturity that enabled them to resist the frosts. Nevertheless all truly tropical species, regardless of how sheltered their locations, were eliminated by these severe cold spells. The final result was loss of approximately half of the species with which we were experimenting.

As far as the palms are concerned, there are other palms growing in tropical countries at elevations above the 5,000-foot level which are well worth testing for their adaptability to Southern California. They might prove of considerable value in landscaping. The most likely ones to thrive here would be those which are native to the western slopes of the South American Andes. It was my earnest desire to undertake a collecting trip to that region in those years, but somehow pressure of duties at the ranch prevented allocation of enough time for the venture.

Mr. Huntington was greatly interested in all the details of improving and developing his ranch. Though he lived in Los Angeles at the Jonathan Club, he took every opportunity to come out to San Marino Ranch to see what progress was being made. While there, he would always watch the workmen with interest and never hesitated to make any suggestions that he believed of practical value. Gardening operations attracted him and he would watch them by the hour, even in the midst of the cloud of dust they would raise at times. Often when he grew tired of leaning on his cane for support, he would search about for something to sit on—a board, a box, or anything that proved handy. If he was thirsty he would kneel down and drink from a nearby hydrant just as his workmen did.

He was a lover of horses and drove a fine pair of chestnut browns to an open surrey; but it was not long before he purchased an automobile as a convenient and faster mode of travel between Los Angeles and his varied interests in California. About once a week he would stay overnight with his close friend and next-door neighbor, George S. Patton. Invariably, the morning following his arrival, weather permitting, he would take a long walk before breakfast to some part of the ranch. Many a time I have met him as early as 6 A.M. walking about and enjoying himself among his beloved oak trees. He would then return to the Patton home for breakfast and later he and his host would board the electric car for their respective offices in the Pacific Electric Building in Los Angeles.

It was on one of these early morning walks that we met at the pumping plant. I was about to descend to the bottom of the shaft when someone behind me said "good morning," and inquired as to what I was doing out so early. It was Mr. Huntington, and I explained that I had planned to inspect the pump. He urged me to continue down the shaft and assured me that he would wait. As I stepped off the last step of the vertical ladder onto the floor of the shaft I touched the fore-part of a striped, furry animal and soon discovered that three visitors had preceded me on this particular visit. I muttered a few unkind words and in record time climbed the forty steps of the ladder to fresh air. Here I was greeted by Mr. Huntington, who was heartily laughing at the episode. I excused myself and went home to change my clothes, meanwhile trying to determine how a family of three skunks could have taken up their abode at the bottom of a forty-foot shaft. This problem was never solved.

We managed to remove this unwelcome family in a completely unique fashion: into the shaft we lowered a three-foot pipe six inches in diameter, one end of which was attached to a rope, the other being blocked by a piece of sturdy burlap. After throwing countless rocks down into the shaft, the three inseparable skunks took refuge in the pipe and in this manner we hoisted them to the surface. After quickly blocking the open end of the pipe with an additional piece of burlap, we transported to more appropriate living quarters the undesirable trio.

[10]

THE OLD SHORB ROAD

Near the citrus orchard, 1896. Photograph by A. C. Vroman

ENTRANCE TO SHORB ESTATE

Looking west from a location now represented by the intersection of San Marino Avenue and Euston Road. Dated: 1905

LILY PONDS ON THE HUNTINGTON ESTATE, *as they appeared in 1906*

LILY PONDS ON THE HUNTINGTON ESTATE, *in 1916, with view of residence*

Early stage of improvements to combine water storage and a bird refuge

COMPLETE LANDSCAPING *which combined water storage and a bird refuge, about 1917-20*
(Above and on opposite page)

later filled in to enlarge the cactus gardens

CANYON ON SHORB ESTATE, *later developed into the*
Japanese Garden

COAT OF ARMS OF THE REPUBLIC OF SAN MARINO
(In carved wooden panel above the fireplace in Shorb house)

THE OLD SHORB RESIDENCE, 1890
Note two millstones, near the hitching post, from the Old Mill.
From photograph in possession of Mr. N. Strain of San Gabriel

ENTRANCE TO CANYON PROPERTY. *Overhanging vines on trees are California wild grape vines*

Early stages of the gardens in 1909, showing large palm moved from
Los Angeles and the residence under construction

ASIATIC DATE PALM

(Phoenix rupicola) *in foreground*

HYBRID DATE PALM

(Between the species from the Canary Islands and the date palm from Arabia)

SLIM-TRUNKED AFRICAN DATE PALM

(Phoenix reclinata)

SOUTH AMERICAN QUEEN PALM

(Arecastrum Romanzoffianum)

CEREUS HUNTINGTONIANUS
Named for Mr. Huntington. The author stands beside it

EARLY STAGES IN THE DEVELOPMENT OF THE CACTUS GARDEN

Above: in the spring of 1910. Below: two years later

TELEGRAPH POLE PLANT (Idria columnaris) *of Lower California*

MAMMILLARIA
COMPRESSA

Commonly known as
pin-cushion cactus

MAMMILLARIA COLLECTION

NIGHT-BLOOMING CEREUS

(Cereus Dayamii). *Opening during the night, the blossoms generally close early in the morning, except on foggy days*

FLOWERS
Of giant night-blooming Cereus glaucus

FRUIT *of night-blooming*
Cereus horridus, var. macrocarpa

THE LATH HOUSE

The first building constructed to house and display rare semi-tropical plants

Above: Partial view of exterior

At right and on opposite page: Portion of interior, showing rare specimen plants

SOME OF THE TREES MOVED WITHIN THE ESTATE ABOUT 1908
Above: Date palm (foreground), first tree moved and the one which crushed the wagon

Left: CEDRUS DEODARA, *one of the four largest trees moved*

Right: ARAUCARIA COOKII, *a rare New Caledonia cone-bearing tree*

The Cactus Garden

Just as the grading for the palm garden began to take shape, I requested permission to establish a cactus garden. Mr. Huntington evidenced complete surprise and questioned why I thought anyone could possibly be interested in such a garden, admitting that he himself thoroughly disliked all types of cacti. His dislike was readily understandable when he explained that it all dated back to the time he had supervised construction work for the Southern Pacific Railroad on the Arizona desert: while backing away from some grading equipment that was passing by, he had had his first painful and never-to-be-forgotten introduction to the prickly cactus.

The conversation about this took place one Sunday afternoon as we were seated in the shade of a group of sycamore trees located in about the middle of the present cactus garden. I explained to Mr. Huntington that Southern California's climatic conditions would be most advantageous toward assembling such a collection, which should include species and varieties from the entire continent. I also pointed out that this planting would be unique, made up solely of a family of American plants which would have definite scientific and therefore educational value. If he should care to extend the plan still further, I suggested, we could include other desert plants such as the yuccas, agaves, dasylirions, and echeverias. And I proposed that we even consider plants from deserts other than American: for example, the South African succulents, such as aloes, euphorbias, crassulas, cotyledons, and mesembryanthemums.

Mr. Huntington finally evinced some real interest in the subject and the proposition, enough to question me as to where such a collection might be planted, such a garden's estimated cost of construction, collection and maintenance, and other pertinent questions. We were sitting where we overlooked a barren hillside that had always been unsightly and unsuitable for most plantings because the soil was worn out; yet this hillside bordered the main drive and was very much in evidence. So I suggested that this spot would be an ideal location for the proposed cactus garden. Mr. Huntington became genuinely interested and soon agreed to the idea, provided that the planting could be arranged to avoid further erosion.

Permission was granted, thereupon, to start a cactus garden on a small scale only, for he was still not convinced about the advisability of planting the entire area to such a garden. As a result, within a short time I obtained an assortment of about 300 plants for the first planting of the collection, and with this showing Mr. Huntington was pleased and satisfied. The actual initial planting, which I did personally with the aid of a few Mexican laborers who spoke little English, was exceptionally gratifying. In spite of the handicaps experienced, that first day's work was quite impressive to us all, including the Mexican workers, who were delighted to see so many plants from their own country.

I began then in earnest to collect plants from the nearby California deserts. Shortly an opportunity presented itself to make a sizeable addition to the collection from the Zobelein Estate; and in scouting about Southern California I located about a dozen more large specimens. The collection was growing rapidly. During those first few years I found myself competing with other collectors. One in particular was Arthur Letts of Hollywood, who was assembling a collection of cactus as part of the landscaping plan to improve the grounds of his new home.

In the summer of 1908 I began a series of collecting trips through the Arizona deserts, collecting about three carloads of very fine specimens. Included among the latter was one carload of young *sahuaros* (the giant cactus *Carnegiea gigantea*), state flower of Arizona. I shall never forget this first trip of mine to that region because of the weather conditions experienced, the mode of transportation, which left much to be desired in comparison with modern comforts, and the one and only encounter with a rattlesnake during all of my collection trips.

The cactus garden, meanwhile, was taking shape much more rapidly than we had expected, and Mr. Huntington took great pleasure in showing his friends about. Mexico is a region where more cactus can be found than in any comparable area in the world, and when I went there on a trip some years later, the assembling of several thousand plants from that region included species and varieties not only of cacti but also of other interesting succulents. Most of this collection was procured directly from the desert, but the rest I obtained from private and commercial sources.

An incident that amused us occurred in Central Mexico while I was selecting a few very desirable specimens of echinocactus (*i.e.,* the barrel cactus) for display purposes, selecting them for size, shape, and color of their spines. When the Mexicans, who had been engaged to transport them from the desert by burros, found it difficult to handle the specimens because of their sharp spines, they put their machetes to use in cutting off the spines. Mr. Huntington was greatly pleased with the results of my Mexican trip, and watched the planting of the specimens in the garden. I found later that the personal contacts I had made while in Mexico were very gratifying, in that they led to additional acquisitions, thus augmenting the collection to such an extent that it became an exceptionally fine representation of North American cactus and other plants known as succulents.

The Border Fence

When I first came to the ranch, the grounds were enclosed by a simple wire fence attached to redwood posts. To improve its appearance, we planted about 350 selected climbing roses along Huntington Drive and San Marino Avenue. The public, however, began to help itself not only to the roses when in bloom, but also to long branches which we were trying to train on the fence. To discourage this habit of appropriation, we planted 200 single pink and white Cherokee roses, which are very decorative but very thorny and, consequently, less useful for ornamental purposes. This expedient proved highly successful and in time the fence was covered, presenting every spring a floral display to be enjoyed by all who passed by. Unhappily, the widening of Huntington Drive eliminated the fence itself, which was later replaced, along the set-back line, by a combination wall and fence.

The Collis P. Huntington Home in San Francisco Destroyed

In April 1906 an incident occurred that brought evidence of deep concern and worry to Mr. Huntington's features, which usually displayed a cheerfulness and optimism toward all with whom he came in contact on his ranch. The San Francisco earthquake and the fire which followed in its wake destroyed the beautiful home of Mrs. Collis P. Huntington with all its treasures, including paintings by such masters as Van Dyck and Rembrandt.

This disaster caused Mr. Huntington much thought on a new subject; structural problems in this part of the country were apparently to be considered gravely in the light of such unpredictable cataclysms of nature. Undoubtedly even at that time plans for the residence on the ranch were taking shape in his mind. Well do I remember one evening when he and I were sitting near the old Shorb house after he had learned of the loss of the mansion on Nob Hill in San Francisco. He remarked to me for the first time that he would build here a home substantial enough to withstand both fire and earthquake, and one which would ultimately prove an asset to the people of California. The realization of this vision is now a part of California's rich heritage. He mentioned at that time also the possibility of erecting a hospital of similarly sound construction.

The Old Shorb Residence

The home of J. de Barth Shorb, former owner of San Marino Ranch, was erected in 1878, a typical California Victorian style, marked by high ceilings and extensive and wide verandas. The interior contained some very fine workmanship of carved wood; particular examples were the mantels above the fireplaces. On the oakwood mantel in the dining room the coat-of-arms of the Republic of San Marino was carved. Mr. Shorb had named his ranch "San Marino" to perpetuate the name that his grandfather had bestowed on a plantation owned by him in Frederick County, Maryland. His grandfather, in turn, had adopted this name from the Republic of San Marino, a small, independent state located in the mountains of Italy.

The decision to dismantle the old house came late in 1906. One particularly curious note of interest to contemporaries of the mid-twentieth century, when comforts are considered necessities rather than luxuries, is the fact that most of the bath tubs and wash basins in this old residence were constructed of wood and lined with sheet zinc —quite a contrast to the shining, durable surfaces of today. Much of the salvaged material made available through the process of dismantling was used in the construction of cottages so badly needed by some of the workmen, many of whom lived in surrounding cities and towns, viz., Pasadena, Alhambra, Lamanda Park, and Los Angeles.

Enough lumber was salvaged to set up the framework for six four-room cottages immediately. During subsequent years more material was acquired through Mr. Huntington's other purchases in this region, chiefly in the San Gabriel Valley.

In 1907 and 1909, respectively, two five-room cottages were added and a twenty-six-room dormitory was erected to accommodate single men. In addition to these dwellings, located south of Huntington Drive, there could also be found on the ranch grounds stables, hay barns, tool and implement sheds, as well as another six-room house for the ranch foreman and several smaller ones for the ranch laborers. This small settlement was known as Krugerville, a name of no special significance but bestowed by the workers.

Mr. Huntington's interest in his newly acquired ranch embraced many of the homely details connected with its management. For example, he took great interest in the farm implements; and a point of special concern was that of transportation vehicles.

Such needs included wagons, buggies, carriages—in all of which he took a personal interest, especially as far as their proper selection was concerned. I remember needing a new buggy at one time, in which to drive around the ranch; when Mr. Huntington knew of the need, he made an appointment to meet me at his Los Angeles office. From there we drove to one of the city's wholesale houses on Los Angeles Street, and as we looked over the stock he pointed out the good and bad features of the various makes. As a consequence of this careful appraisal our final selection proved to be a very durable piece of equipment. Many were the rides we took together in this very buggy, on our inspection tours of Mr. Huntington's various landholdings.

Some years after this, when Mr. Huntington and his second wife had moved into their new residence I met Mrs. Huntington with her companion, Miss Campbell; they were trying to locate Mr. Huntington. Learning from me where he could be found, Mrs. Huntington requested that I drive them to the place. The conveyance, as was proved, was not built to bear the strain of additional passengers, so before we reached our destination, the seat spring broke with such a bang that it frightened both women. We continued, however, until we reached the spot where Mr. Huntington and his secretary were watching a crew of workmen mixing concrete. Mrs. Huntington quickly said, as soon as her husband came within range to hear, "Edward, help me out of this contraption!" adding with some feeling, "It is just about time you provided Hertrich with a more modern piece of equipment. Why don't you buy him an automobile?" And so he did, shortly after this occurrence. The ladies would not accept my offer to drive them home; a chauffeur was sent with the open car to take them back to the house.

Sunday Afternoon Visits to the Ranch

Before his home was built at San Marino, Mr. Huntington lived at the Jonathan Club in Los Angeles, but he invariably spent Sundays and holidays on the ranch. Generally we would walk about the premises, or sit under the oak trees, talking over future plans and contemplated improvements of his properties. Often he would recount stories of his early life: how he began working in a small hardware store as a youngster, saving the greater portion of his earnings; how, later, he applied for the position of clerk in the large hardware firm of Sargent in New York and was informed that the only opening was a porter's job. He accepted this place and within a few months' time he had been promoted to a clerical position.

It was during one of his Fourth of July visits, when we were walking through a field of shocked hay, that we discovered a fire, started by firecrackers thrown abroad by boys in the neighborhood. It was rapidly creeping toward the hay shocks. I hurriedly broke off a few small limbs of a nearby shrub with which to beat out the fire. Mr. Huntington quickly removed his coat and used it to smother some of the mounting flames.

One very warm Sunday afternoon we walked toward the stable, passing the water-tank tower. Mr. Huntington called my attention to a wet streak, evident the full length of the tower, commenting that there must be a leak in the water tank. Climbing the tower, I was unable to locate any leak. The next morning, after closer examination, I was surprised to find that the wet streak had been caused by melted honey which to all appearances had been stored up there for many years. We removed the inside boards of the water tower and found great quantities of honey everywhere we looked. Removing it, we found so much that it filled every container available, including washtubs. This supply was distributed to the employees on the ranch, enough to last everyone at least two years.

"Take It Off the Old Man's Bill"

All through the first year of my association with Mr. Huntington, I was aware that he was most watchful of all my actions and my business dealings with others. This careful scrutiny was due, I learned, to the fact that my predecessor on this particular job had been somewhat dilatory in the discharge of his duties, and also was a man of doubtful integrity. It was some time before Mr. Huntington was thoroughly convinced of my honesty, but once I had attained his confidence it was a great pleasure to work for him.

Many opportunities presented themselves whereby I could have made a percentage on a sale. I recollect one transaction in particular which amounted to seven hundred dollars. The party in question offered me 15 per cent commission on completion of the sale. I declined to accept it, but suggested that he deduct this amount "from the Old Man's bill." About two years later, while discussing costs of certain items with

Mr. Huntington, some of which seemed excessively high, there was occasion for me to remark jokingly that thus far I'd not accepted any personal commissions on any items. With a sheepish smile he commented, "I know, Hertrich, instead you've had it 'deducted from the Old Man's bill.' "

The Lath House

It became apparent in the early days when we first began to collect palms and cactus plants that we needed a place to store such specimens for observation, as well as an adequate place to establish some of them before planting out in the open garden. With these needs in mind, I suggested to Mr. Huntington that we erect a lath house large enough not only to store plants for interim periods, but also to accommodate enough for display purposes in the category of ornamental shade-loving plants. I then submitted sketches of a lath house three hundred feet long, designed with a center fulcrum in circular form measuring one hundred feet in diameter, the two arms extending east and west, each fifty feet wide. From the floor to the top of the circular dome the measurement was thirty-five feet.

After the plans were sufficiently developed, I engaged a local carpenter and together we worked out the design, which proved to be something new in the way of lath-house construction. Timber was set in concrete and the redwood slats eighteen feet long were ideal for arching the dome. When completed there were planted in this lath house all types of ferns initially, and they included some rare species from Australia, New Zealand, Mexico, and Central America. For Mrs. Huntington's pleasure as well as that of her friends, displays were made of many flowering plants—cyclamens, primulas, azaleas, rhododendrons and others.

Soon after completing this structure, I procured a fine specimen of Australian tree fern, which at that time was considered more or less of a novelty. Mr. Huntington was very much intrigued by its grace and beauty and asked me to plant others about the place. Although they were difficult to secure, I finally obtained a few species from horticultural establishments, some from the Plath Fern Nursery in San Francisco, others from William F. Dreer, Philadelphia, and from W. A. Manda, South Orange, New Jersey. Meanwhile I began to raise about two hundred plants from spores, all of which were planted under the large oaks north of the residence or in the canyon.

Transplanting Large Trees

Mr. Huntington early expressed his desire to have the gardens surrounding his proposed new home appear as mature as possible from the very beginning, and he inquired of me if it would be possible to transplant large trees. I was willing to make the attempt, but I undertook this task with the most primitive equipment and with a crew of men totally inexperienced as far as this type of work was concerned. Mr. Huntington himself was very soon aware of the fact that moving large specimens with the tools and labor available made the job doubly hard.

We transplanted desirable trees from wherever they could be found; some of them stood from thirty to fifty feet high and weighed from ten to twenty tons apiece. Since Mr. Huntington owned properties scattered throughout Los Angeles County, many of the large palms were taken from great distances to be planted on the ranch. The former Childs estate, between Eleventh and Twelfth streets and Main and Broadway in Los Angeles, was the source of some of the finest specimens.

Lack of trucks, tractors, and modern lifting equipment, however, slowed down the work to a great extent, and I spent many a sleepless night devising a plan that might successfully transport and transplant some huge tree on which we had set our minds. One medium-sized palm tree, though finally transplanted with success, involved us in an experience that was almost disastrous. It was located on one of the many Huntington-owned lots in South Pasadena. After it was properly dug, boxed, and loaded on the strongest wagon available, we proceeded along the road until we encountered, at one of the street intersections along Huntington Drive, a shallow stone gutter. As the front wheels hit the gutter, the axle snapped, and the result can be imagined. We completely blocked the intersection, much to the disgust of both the police and the general public. In the first place, it had been very difficult to load the palm onto the wagon, but this effort could not be compared with the work entailed in transferring the same cargo from a broken wagon to another conveyance. Meanwhile numerous curious citizens had gathered about to watch us and offered endless as well as many useless bits of advice. This experience, we later realized, was only a mild example of the worries that were in store for us during the coming year, though I'd actually begun to believe that most of my troubles had been overcome, with the favorable results we had had in moving some very fine specimens during the months succeeding our initial experiments.

The next large palm to be moved was located on a lot at 19th and Main Streets in Los Angeles. This experience was to prove almost fatal to one of the workmen and myself. After boxing the large specimen we had proceeded to raise it to the surface out of its hole, with regular house-moving jacks. Suddenly the ground beneath two of the jacks caved in, throwing the palm to one side. Only quick instinctive action saved the two of us from being crushed against the bank by the weight of the heavy palm. Later examination proved that an old cesspool was located in that particular spot and that the top of it had caved in under the weight of our jacks.

Various methods were adopted in transporting large specimens like the one mentioned above: some we were able to load on trucks pulled by horses; others we loaded on flat cars and delivered to a spur track at the ranch which had been provided by the Pacific Electric Railway. By this time I considered myself a seasoned tree-mover, but soon I realized that there was much more to be learned. We decided at one time to move a beautiful specimen of a palm from its location on top of a knoll near East Lake Park (now known as Lincoln Park), Los Angeles. It was a Canary Island date palm and we resolved to move it in an upright position in order to avoid damaging its beautiful long fronds. As may be imagined, it was not easily accessible at the very start; but we managed to box it, excavating on the incline, and then proceeded to pull it to the surface with cable and capstan. In the process, the chain around the box snapped; it flung back and hit me across the forehead, and I "blacked out." Following a forced intermission on this account, we proceeded to load the palm on an especially wide truck loaned to us by the Los Angeles Railway Company. After negotiating the heavy load down the steep hill, we believed our worries to be over. The trip through the next street, however, which was several blocks long, gravely hindered progress because of many soft places in the street that had been occasioned by recent excavations.

At one place all four wheels of the truck sank to the hubs and we had to resort to capstan and cable again to pull the truck back onto solid ground. To anchor the capstan we were obliged to dig a hole in the street, which, of course, was an absolute violation of the law. Suddenly and most unexpectedly the street inspector drove up in a buggy and asked to see my permit authorizing me to dig a hole in a city street. Since I did not have one, he requested that I accompany him to his office. En route to the office we passed a saloon and I offered him a drink, which he accepted. We talked things over while we drank and soon compromised our difficulties. He pointed out that although my employer, Mr. Huntington, owned a great deal of land, this definitely did not include the city streets! So I solemnly promised not to dig any more holes in the streets without first obtaining a permit.

By that time the afternoon was well spent and, returning to the truck, I decided to leave it overnight on the side street, sending the men and wagons home with the understanding that they were to report back early the next morning so we could finish the transportation of the palm. A return trip was also necessary that night in order to place a warning lantern on the truck. The following day we made good progress on the highway, but as we were crossing the Southern Pacific Railroad tracks, the upper leaves of this tall palm pushed a pair of telephone wires upward until they contacted the high-tension electric wires. Fireworks really began!—scaring everyone, including the eight horses pulling the truck. The center leaves of the palm were severely burned and everyone who saw it was of the opinion that it wouldn't grow after receiving such a shock. But it survived and is still growing.

During 1907 and 1908 we transplanted some of the largest of the trees already established on the ranch to make room for the new home, plans for which were taking shape at the time. These trees included a huge camphor; a very large *Magnolia grandiflora* with twin trunks; one of the magnificent Deodar cedars (*Cedrus deodara*); a tall Tasmanian Dammar pine (*Agathis robusta*); and an Australian bunya-bunya tree known botanically as *Araucaria Bidwilli,* planted in 1908, one of the pine family, a relative of which (*A. Cookii*) is pictured in the accompanying pages. Each of these specimens weighed between fifteen and twenty tons. The agathis was about forty feet tall and presented a peculiar problem of transplanting: it had very few side roots but a long tap root seven inches in diameter. We were obliged to cut this tap root five feet below the ground's surface, and then we seared the cut with a plumber's blow-torch to stop the bleeding. I was skeptical about the success of moving this tree, but it turned out satisfactorily and is still growing.

From San Diego I once procured a number of the tall *Cocos plumosa* palms, which we loaded onto flat cars and which were delivered to the spur track at the ranch, a very satisfactory arrangement. On their arrival, Mr. Huntington asked that the unloading be delayed long enough for him to take a few pictures of them. Two of the last large palms moved at this time were brought down from San Francisco for sentimental reasons: they had stood near the Collis P. Huntington home which had been destroyed by the earthquake and fire of 1906. Although the leaves of both these palms had been completely burned and the trunks charred, they began to grow again the following year and by 1910 had wholly recovered.

Whenever we were engaged in planting these large specimens, Mr. Huntington would watch the procedure with evident interest and often with deep concern. On one occasion, standing close to the scene of operations—as he always did—a small piece of timber flew past his face, missing him by inches. A few minutes later he merely said "good night" and walked away without so much as mentioning the close disaster.

[36]

A Trip with Mr. Huntington

In those early days I made frequent trips to nurseries where desirable material could be found to incorporate in our gardens here. These nurseries were located chiefly in San Jose, San Francisco, and San Diego. One day when I commented to Mr. Huntington that I was planning to go to San Diego shortly, he immediately replied that he had to go to San Diego to look over some land and proposed that we should go together.

On the appointed day we met in Los Angeles and boarded the morning train, expecting to arrive in San Diego about 1:00 P.M. Promptly at twelve noon, Mr. Huntington took a paper sack out of his handbag. The sack contained two sandwiches and two bananas, which he divided with me, remarking that we could save time by eating our lunch then instead of later. During the ensuing conversation, Mr. Huntington asked the name of the hotel that I generally patronized. I advised him that it was a moderately priced family hotel known as the Brewster. Said he, "We shall both go there."

When we reached San Diego he accompanied me to the Sessions Nursery, where I ordered a considerable quantity of plant material; and then he went on alone to finish his own business while I visited two more nurseries. We met again at the hotel at six o'clock and together went to a local restaurant for our evening meal. Having had breakfast at six in the morning, and the very light lunch at noon, I had a tremendous appetite by this time and ordered an extensive meal consisting of soup, Hungarian goulash, dumplings, vegetables, apple pie, and a stein of beer. Mr. Huntington duplicated that order for himself.

The following morning, Colonel Ed Fletcher, I believe it was, called for us and drove us over a large section of San Diego County. At one point where we stopped we met Mr. Scripps, of newspaper fame. Returning to San Diego at the end of the day, we boarded the evening train for home. This was one of many trips we made together throughout Southern California in the early days, sometimes by railroad but often by automobile.

On one trip when Mr. Huntington was obliged to attend a meeting of Southern Pacific Railroad officials in Santa Barbara I accompanied him. After the meeting, we visited some of the larger estates in Montecito—places of rare beauty for the horticulturist. Some of our experiences while traveling by automobile in those days stay indelibly in my memory. On one trip to San Bernardino County we bogged down into an irrigation ditch and I was obliged to walk to a nearby farm to secure a team of horses to pull the heavy car out onto solid ground. That particular day was an unlucky one for us. About thirty minutes later, while driving along a very narrow road from Colton to Riverside, the chauffeur failed to slow down while crossing an irrigation flume that was projecting above the surface of the road. The sudden impact bounced both of us right up to the roof of the car: one very noticeable result was that Mr. Huntington's square-top derby was crushed flatter than the proverbial pancake.

First Avocado Orchard in Southern California

Shortly after I began the task of improving San Marino Ranch, Mr. Huntington came up to me one day and showed me a handful of seeds that he had been carrying in his pocket. He asked me if I knew what they were. I recognized the misnamed "alligator pear" seeds as avocado seeds. He explained that he had first eaten the fruit at the Jonathan Club and had enjoyed it so much that he had asked the chef for all the seeds he had. He gave me the seeds and questioned the possibility of growing the trees on the ranch. Feeling confident that we would have a measure of success with them, I planted the seeds immediately in pots and set about collecting more from both Mr. Huntington's acquaintances and mine throughout Los Angeles and Orange counties. In three months' time we had accumulated some three hundred seeds.

Little did we know at the time that the small handful of avocado seeds brought from the Jonathan Club kitchen would become the nucleus of the first avocado orchard in Southern California. When the young plants had attained a height of several feet they were transplanted to the field in orchard form, *i.e.*, twenty-five feet apart both ways. We continued this performance as the seedlings developed until in 1907 we had seven acres planted to avocado trees. Then as soon as they had become well established in the field we began to bud them to whatever varieties were available. This was a long process, since buds of good varieties were exceedingly scarce in those days.

Mr. Huntington was very proud of this orchard that he was personally responsible for starting, and took every opportunity to show visitors the results of his unique method of collecting seeds with which to start his avocado planting. Some of the seed produced outstanding specimens which are still standing and worthy of that designation even today, in 1949; some have attained a height of fifty feet and a spread of about the same, with trunks averaging three feet in diameter. There were richly flavored Mexican varieties which he favored more than others from the point of view of the epicure; but realizing that the larger, less rich varieties were better for commercial use, he encouraged the budding of the latter.

Our hopes for the success of this new orchard were considerably dashed the winter of 1913. On the sixth and seventh of January the low temperatures of 20° and 22° Fahrenheit were recorded two nights in succession: this was cold enough to freeze all the young seedlings in the ground. We were mightily discouraged by this turn of events and concluded that our experiment was a failure due to lack of more suitable location. The following spring, to my great surprise, new growth was discovered beneath the soil surface on almost all the young trees. We nursed them along, nurturing the young shoots for two years, and then rebudded the entire orchard to available varieties.

The immediate aftermath of that freeze was a source of some embarrassment to me when the family arrived in Southern California the following winter. Apparently Mr. Huntington had informed Mrs. Collis P. Huntington about the new avocado venture, because upon my first introduction to her she inquired about the progress of the well-being of the trees raised from seed collected and planted by Mr. Huntington. At that particular time, all we had to show for our efforts were the remnants of the frozen orchard. And to make matters worse, the price of avocados rose that January of 1914 to $1.50 apiece!

Family Fruit Orchard

It was back in 1907 that Mr. Huntington suggested the planting of what he called the family fruit orchard. We selected a location about 250 yards east of the proposed new residence. The area was large enough to accommodate all kinds of fruit and berries that could be grown in the Southern California climate. We first planted six trees each of grapefruit, and of navel and Valencia oranges; three each of tangerines, mandarins, blood oranges, the foreign St. Michaels, and the Oriental kumquats. Later we added three plants each of the Mission and Kadota figs; four apricots and nectarines; eight peaches of different varieties; six varieties of plums; a few cherries, walnuts, sapotas, and cherimoyas; and about a dozen guavas.

Gophers and Squirrels

In the early days on the ranches, the control of rodents, particularly gophers and ground squirrels, had been neglected. As a result there were great losses to all kinds of farm crops. At the time I was placed in charge of the ranch properties, I concentrated first on the extermination of the worst offenders. I purchased a gross of gopher traps and engaged a young, intelligent Mexican to devote his entire time to this work. He set out one morning with 25 traps, and for the required subsequent days followed the same procedure until all the traps had been used. From that time on it took all of his time simply to check and reset these traps over a period of three years.

For the first year, the average catch per month was 364 gophers; the second year, the average was lowered to 200 per month, and the third year, still less. During the fourth year we found that only half of the young man's time was needed for satisfactory control, and finally the time spent on this project was diminished to an average of two hours daily. All these years, our young workman was required to bring back daily the tails of all gophers he had trapped.

Mr. Huntington became very much interested in this proceeding. One day when we met the boy coming in with the traps hanging over his shoulders, Mr. Huntington remarked to me, "It is too bad these are not moles. We could start a fur business."

It was about 1906 that Mr. Huntington sent a pair of gray squirrels to the ranch from Mt. Lowe. He had watched them at the tavern, noticing how tame they had become with the guests. We prepared a cage for them in the top of one of the large oak trees. After the squirrels had been placed in their new home, a man was sent daily to provide them with food and water. After approximately six months' time we set them free and for a full year they disappeared. The following spring, however, baby squirrels were much in evidence and from that time on, their numbers increased to such an extent that after about fifteen years we were obliged to resort to control measures. They became very destructive and later they moved into neighboring territory, as far north as Oak Knoll and south towards San Gabriel. The supply of food that they relished was ample on the ranch: pecans, walnuts, acorns, various palm seeds; and they also ate avocados and other fruits of various kinds.

In 1912 when I received a shipment of birds from New York, a pair of red fox squirrels was included. Unfortunately the female died en route. The male we housed in a regular squirrel cage, but he was not very happy so I turned him free. That was the last we ever saw of him. However, he made his presence known by a strange set of offspring which looked just like the other squirrels of the neighborhood—all gray—except that the newcomers had red tails!

Increased Responsibilities

When I accepted the position with Mr. Huntington it was with the understanding that I was to be the landscape gardener exclusively. Scott White, the ranch foreman, was in full charge of the citrus orchards and other farm lands. This was a very satisfactory arrangement and lasted about two years, at the end of which time Mr. Huntington requested that I assume additional responsibility. A little at a time, I was directed to take over the supervision of the ranch work, including the citrus groves, and all grading and excavating in connection with the gardens and buildings. At first, this embraced only part of the extensive San Marino Ranch—viz., that which lay north of Huntington Drive; but at Mr. White's retirement I was offered the superintendency of all the properties in San Marino, which included the home ranch, El Molino Ranch, and the Winston, Titus, and Heslop properties.

It soon became evident that I was to take over the supervision of the citrus packinghouse as well and to use it exclusively for the packing of fruit gathered from the Huntington property. During the readjustment period, I was able to place Sam Cockrell as foreman of the San Marino Ranch; L. H. Brummet as foreman of El Molino Ranch; and William Beckman as manager of the citrus packinghouse. Receiving full co-operation from all these men enabled us to realize a successful program. Furthermore, the increased responsibilities brought new enjoyment in my work, for I was able to bring about the substitution of modern methods for old-fashioned types of ranching. In many instances favorable returns reflected the soundness of the different approach.

At the time I took over the citrus groves, the production per acre was considerably below the average. According to packinghouse records, the orchards owned by Mr. Huntington and the Huntington Land and Improvement Company were near the bottom of the list of fifteen growers in the vicinity, both as to quantity and grade of fruit. In a few years' time we were gratified to find that these same orchards had climbed nearly to the top of the list on both counts. The actual production per acre was rising so astonishingly that shortly Mr. Huntington asked me to plant 75 to 100 additional acres to Valencia oranges.

About 1912 we rebudded some twenty acres of comparatively unproductive navel trees to Valencias. At the same time I started to make extensive experiments with fertilizers and improved cultural methods, as well as to keep individual tree records on small test plots. Later on, I extended the records to ten acres, and soon after assuming responsibility for all of the groves I introduced similar methods there. A final effort to establish an accurate record that would form the basis for increased production involved the keeping of individual records on eighteen thousand trees, noting various methods of fertilizing, over a period of four years, 1916-1919. Using these records, I prepared colored charts indicating the numbers and locations of the trees that were bearing well or poorly, and thus I was able to present a clear picture of the existing situation. This proved to be of great value later in initiating corrective measures.

One of our orchards was located near a gopher-infested alfalfa field. We had noted that a great many of the trees in this area were in poor condition and that the yield was very low; but it was not until some time later that we discovered the damage was due to gophers eating at the roots. Another plot, five acres in dimension, which was producing poorly was found to have been planted over non-perforative subsoil; and still another ten acres was planted to Valencias rebudded on lemon tops, a large percentage of the trees being afflicted with bark blisters. Scattered through the entire orchard, drone trees could be found: these are apparently healthy specimens but poor in production. Many of the latter we were able to rebud from high-producing trees of good quality fruit.

During the period when I was making fertilizer experiments, I selected one twenty-five-acre plot of young Valencia trees and applied fertilizer in liquid form only. At the highest point of the orchard I had built a concrete tank fifty feet long, six feet wide, four feet high. This was filled about three-quarters full with dairy fertilizer and water added to the top. The upper end of the tank was connected to the water supply line while the opposite end joined the irrigating flow, both lines controlled by valves. During irrigating time the outlet valve was opened to mix the liquid manure with the irrigation water. About twice a year we added commercial fertilizer to the concrete tank. As a result of this method of fertilizing, which was a radical change over the formerly accepted way, the young trees grew noticeably faster, had dark green, lush foliage, and came into good fruition from one to two years sooner than trees on any of the other plots. This experiment would have been interesting to continue for an added number of years in order to form a more definite conclusion; but unfortunately it was brought to a sudden end by the sale of the entire block. Sir Joseph Duveen acquired this land as part payment in a trade for art objects, chiefly paintings, which Mr. Huntington had just purchased.

FORMAL ROSE PERGOLA *from northwest corner of residence*

ROSE GARDEN AT TWO STAGES, *in 1918 (above), and at its best in 1920 (below)*

ROSE GARDEN *in process of development*

SPRING FLOWERING ANNUALS AND BULBS *in the rose garden*

BROADEST SPREADING OAK TREE
ON THE ESTATE

*Located between the library and the art gallery
buildings, about 170 years old. In 1918 it measured
136 feet in spread.*

MR. HUNTINGTON *resting on one of the oak trees saved by tree surgery*

FIRST EXTENSIVE TREE
SURGERY

*Practiced on a fallen oak which still
flourishes in the garden. Aviary in
background*

FIRST PORTION OF AVIARY, *for parrots, other talking birds, and singing birds*

BIRD REFUGE; *also served as water storage for irrigation purposes*

THE RESIDENCE AFTER COMPLETION. *Note joints between red tiles, now painted dark*

The Rose Garden

In the fall of 1907 I submitted to Mr. Huntington a plan for an extensive rose garden to be located west of the proposed new residence. The area consisted of several acres of rolling ground and involved considerable grading and the filling in of a small ravine. Iron arbors were then installed to support climbing roses.

The following January we planted the first selection of bush roses, to be followed by others during succeeding years. The main axis of the garden was planned to coincide with the east-to-west axis of the new house. However, when the time arrived for the erection of the house, Mr. Huntington strenuously objected to the removal of two large oak trees. Therefore changes had to be made to protect and preserve the trees. Such changes not only disturbed the rose garden alignment but also the previously planted North Vista axis: neither one has ever been corrected.

The bush roses acquired had ample time to develop before the family was expected to occupy the home, but my chief concern was the problem of covering the rose arbors. I searched throughout most of the nurseries in California for large specimens in containers and finally located some near San Francisco. At the same time, quite by accident, I found there also the first of our Chinese magnolias which have been grown so successfully ever since. From Mexico some time earlier I had obtained a small bit of seed from a Montezuma cypress (*Taxodium mucronatum*, from Chapultepec Park); four specimens of this formed the key trees in the center of the rose garden.

About 1922 the size of this garden was reduced perhaps 35 per cent by eliminating the eastern portion. This presented the opportunity to camouflage to some extent the conflicting alignments of the residence and garden axes. To remedy the situation still further, several spreading Chinese elms were planted in conjunction with the placing of the Greek temple. In 1938 the garden was changed again when all but the four center rose beds were converted into lawn. By 1946 it was possible to replant much of the former area; one thousand rose bushes were secured, including most of the latest varieties, and are now forming a display garden comparable to that of earlier years.

Oak Trees

One of the first questions Mr. Huntington asked me, when I came to take charge of his ranch, was whether oak trees could be transplanted successfully. His liking for these natives was so great that at one time he threatened to discharge one of the property surveyors who had driven a spike into the trunk of an oak as a surveyor's mark. He wished to use oaks extensively in his landscaping plan, and although at the time I had been told that live oaks generally did not transplant well, I could see no insurmountable difficulty in the matter. Consequently, the following year during the month of February we put through a program of transplanting 650 live oaks from the canyon, ranging in height from five to ten feet, and with bare roots. The trunk caliber in these trees ranged from one to three inches. Of the entire number we finally lost only eighteen. Some of them have now attained great size, depending, of course, upon their location, the type of soil, and amount of water available; they average from fifteen to thirty-six inches in trunk diameter and in spread from forty to sixty feet.

Mr. Huntington took a very special interest in two oaks that had been blown over years before he acquired the property. The trunks of both trees lay flat on the ground with parts of the roots exposed. In each case some of the limbs had been broken in the fall but the tree had assumed an upright position in a valiant effort to resume its natural growth. Decay had caused wide and deep cavities in the trunks and main limbs where fungus had been able to make inroads; but in spite of such handicaps, the foliage appeared healthy and new growth continued to push its way out during spring and summer. This phenomenon so intrigued Mr. Huntington that he began to question how the trees could be saved and inquired about the cost involved in doing the job properly. An estimate of this sort is difficult to arrive at: for one thing, it is impossible to tell from outward appearances how deeply the fungus has penetrated into the hard wood. All affected areas would require chiseling out and the process might be a long one. I made a rough estimate of $500 to $800 per tree; the latter figure proved to be the more correct, and this was in 1906 when labor, including the skilled labor necessary for tree surgery, was far below the present-day wage scale.

The large cavities in the trunk and limbs of the tree received attention first of all: they were thoroughly cleaned, and then filled with concrete and re-enforcing steel rods. To my knowledge this was the first major tree surgery accomplished in Southern California. The operation proved entirely successful and the healing over the concrete fills was complete in about ten or fifteen years. The largest opening to be treated was three feet six inches long by twenty-six inches wide. There was no subject Mr. Hunting-ton loved to discuss with visitors more than the trees he had been able to save, especially this one—located between the residence (now the art gallery) and the rose garden—which is still in good condition today.

One of the other trees treated was the large Engelmann oak located between the art gallery and the library buildings. Neglect had brought it to a state where about 50

per cent of the branches were affected, and it needed immediate attention if the specimen was to be saved as part of the landscaping plan. The other half of the branches
were partially or completely dried and needed removing or at least judicious pruning.
On the whole, this tree was in a very doubtful condition as far as promise of recovery
was concerned. However, under the treatment it was given, within two years' time it
began to show new growth and it recovered enough to become a truly beautiful specimen. In 1919 it received a serious setback when excavation for the new library building
changed the grade alignment and made it necessary to raise the former level under the
tree by thirty inches. This added fill created a situation which was most unnatural—one
which is often fatal to oaks—where lawn or other vegetation is cultivated beneath.
It is only a matter of years until the adverse results of such action must become evident.

The New Residence

E. S. Code, building engineer for a railroad company, first prepared plans for
Mr. Huntington's residence on San Marino Ranch; this was some years before the
firm of Myron Hunt and Elmer Grey of Los Angeles was commissioned to draw the
final plans.

Two sets of pencil sketches dated June 1904 and June 1905, respectively, showed
elevations and floor plans. Basement plans included not only a utility room and a wine
cellar, but also a bowling alley and a gymnasium. The first plans showed a living-
room, drawing-room, den, lanai, a portico, and utility room. On the second floor were
to be seven bedrooms, six baths, a sitting-room, two dressing-rooms, plus seven servants'
rooms and two baths. A large attic consisting of ten rooms provided ample storage
space. The residence as designed by Hunt and Grey embodied most of the ideas
contained in Code's sketches, with the noted exception of the billiard room and the
bowling alley, which were to be accommodated in a separate building.

In the fall of 1908, plans for the new Huntington home were far enough advanced
for me to arrange for the excavation of the large basement to a depth of twelve feet.
Since steam- and gasoline-powered shovels were not available at that time, the job had
to be accomplished with the aid only of horses and plows, scrapers and dump wagons.
The latter had to be loaded by hand. We were obliged to move 8,000 cubic yards of
soil, one half of which was taken out with scrapers and spread close to the homesite.
The balance was largely very poor soil and therefore was hauled by dump wagons to

[53]

a low spot as a fill-in: this area later became part of the cactus garden. It was impressive to Mr. Huntington as well as to other observers to see eight horses hitched to a heavy road plow for the purpose of loosening the remaining two or three feet of hard clay soil in the excavation; for ordinarily, most basement excavations would not be large enough to accommodate a plow, let alone a plow and horses that could be turned about at will.

In October 1908 Carl Leonardt of Los Angeles was awarded the contract for the re-enforced concrete part of the structure, which was expected to be completed by June 1, 1909; additional time was found to be required, however, due to rainy weather and the delayed delivery of necessary building materials. A contract for the interior finishing work—woodcarving, etc.—on the first and second floors was given to Duveen Brothers of New York, London, and Paris, early in 1909. They, in turn, sublet most of it to White, Allom & Company of London and New York. It was Mr. Huntington's wish to have this part of the work completed by January 1, 1910, but delay after delay retarded the progress to such an extent that the architects sent their general super-intendent, J. L. Hillman, to London to help expedite the work. Other unavoidable delays were due to time consumed in corresponding with the various contractors in London, New York, Baltimore, and Los Angeles: the marble work was being done by Evans Marble Company in Baltimore; plumbing fixtures were to be furnished by L. A. Mott Iron Works in New York; while the hardware was being purchased in London, Paris, or New York, as well as in Los Angeles.

Most of the wood finish arrived from London in sealed tin cases, packed in large wooden boxes, during the months of November and December in 1909. Preceding the arrival of this material, Alexander Black and an assistant representing White, Allom & Company arrived from England to supervise the installation of all the material contracted for from that firm. Plastering was supervised by Mr. Bultitude of New York. The second masonry contract was let to Richards-Neustadt of Los Angeles and included the erection and finishing of all exterior and interior walls, exclusive of work covered in the White, Allom & Company contract. Richards-Neustadt was given, as well, the contract to build the garage, the office, bowling alley, stables, and the car house.

Painting the interior was an item that required considerable time because a minimum of six coats was to be applied everywhere: eight coats, however, were applied in most cases, and in a few, ten. All painted surfaces were to be rubbed smooth between coats. The last coat of enamel was rubbed with pumice and rottenstone to produce a satin finish, a truly beautiful achievement.

To facilitate the landscaping adjacent to the home, the general contractor was requested to complete the walls for the terrace and courtyard as soon as humanly possible. This was just another indication of Mr. Huntington's desire for early occupancy of the home.

When the Huntington family finally moved into their new home in January 1914, Mrs. Huntington was well pleased with all that had been done, with a single exception: she definitely objected to the white cement used in the joints between the red imported Welsh tiles on the terrace, loggia, and portico. The joints carefully filled with the white cement gave to her the appearance of a checkerboard; they were subsequently colored to harmonize with the tiles. One mistake in the planning was recognized by all parties concerned. The distance between the butler's pantry and the entrance door at the portico was too great for efficient service. In order to answer the doorbell—a frequent occurrence—a servant was required to walk (and in some instances, to run) the entire length of the main hall which ran east and west, and then through the hall leading north to the portico. This was a fault that could not be remedied.

The Wine Cellar

The northeast section of the vast basement was designated as a wine cellar. Soon after the completion of the basement walls, this section was equipped with racks and doors and other necessary accommodation for the anticipated contents. Considerable amounts of wine had been stored on the premises for several years, in a small shack known to a very few of us. This wine originated in the San Gabriel Winery, which Mr. Huntington had acquired while purchasing a large tract of land that included the winery.

Only the very best and oldest wines were sent to the ranch. These included port, sherry, tokay, sauterne and the noted California wine, zinfandel, as well as a few others. All except a very small portion was stored in barrels and hogsheads. When time came for the transfer of these wines from the shack to the cellar, a holiday was chosen when only a few men were present, so news of the storage was not widely known. About two years later the supply was augmented considerably when we received a shipment of European wines and liquors. From that time on, I was considered custodian-of-the-wine-cellar; this assignment was no novelty to me, since in my younger years I had been active in vineyards, helping to make wine during harvest time and becoming acquainted with its care and storage. I soon learned that the Huntington family used very little of the cellar's contents, but served it generously whenever guests were present.

A Private Railroad Track

For the convenience of car-lot delivery to the San Marino Ranch, when shipments of various kinds and large quantities of materials began to come in, Mr. Huntington had a private spur track installed. It was a branch of the Sierra Madre car line and followed San Marino Avenue north to a point now known as Stratford Avenue, thence west on Stratford to what is now the entrance to the Library grounds. During 1909 and early 1910, when the residence was under construction, the track was extended to the homesite for further convenience in delivering building materials, such as sand, gravel, cement, lumber, and steel, as well as household goods. And again in 1919 and 1920, when the library was being built, the track was extended to that location to facilitate delivery of essential materials. Many shipments, also, of art objects and plant materials passed over this track during the subsequent years, until 1924, when certain alterations involving a new approach to the library necessitated the relocation of the spur farther toward the south.

Mr. Huntington owned three private cars, the "Alabama" in 1913 before his second marriage, and later the "San Marino Number 1" and the "San Marino Number 2." At first the latter were housed in a temporary car shed, but later in a re-enforced concrete building along the side of the spur track. Mr. Huntington used these cars very seldom; when he traveled alone he used Pullman accommodations. But after the completion of the San Marino home, and subsequent to his second marriage, it was the custom for the family to travel in the Number 1 car, while the servants had the use of Number 2, which was a combination passenger and baggage car. It was in the latter that many of the invaluable art treasures and rare books crossed the continent to the Huntington family home in California.

The first arrival of the family at the Santa Fe station proved to be quite a celebrated event. On that day of January 23, 1914, newspaper reporters and photographers were there in great numbers, much to the dismay of Mrs. Huntington, who heartily disliked publicity of any kind. The following year a repetition of this procedure was avoided by scheduling the trip to Pasadena, but having the family leave the train at Lamanda Park. From there Mr. and Mrs. Huntington, Miss Campbell (Mrs. Huntington's companion), and Mr. Huntington's secretary rode to the family home in the limousine, while the servants rode in the touring car. Meanwhile the baggage was allowed to remain in the private car until the car could be switched onto the spur track at the ranch and unloaded there.

[56]

It was in 1911 that the re-enforced concrete car house was built to accommodate these private cars, at a location now represented by the intersection of Oxford and Stratford Roads. Until 1924 it served as a terminal convenient both for the family and for the increasing shipments of building materials and new acquisitions.

Founding the City of San Marino

Ownership not only of the San Marino Ranch, but also of extensive properties known as the Winston, Titus, and Heslop tracts, plus El Molino Ranch, made Mr. Huntington the largest landowner in that section of Los Angeles County which was later to be incorporated as the City of San Marino.

On many occasions Mr. Huntington and I talked over the possibilities of incorporating certain surrounding areas into a city of the sixth class. Such a city, according to his wishes, would include if possible all of his properties in this particular section, and sufficient further land to assure the required number of permanent residents necessary to obtain a charter allowing incorporation, as well as sufficient area for economic administration.

It became my job to check the areas involved, and my particular assignment was to secure evidence of five hundred bona fide residents. The south, west, and part of the north boundaries of the joint properties were considered established by adjacent cities. This left some latitude to the northeast, the east, and the southeast for consideration. A plan of the new city-to-be was drawn up and tentatively agreed to by Mr. Huntington, George S. Patton, W. L. Valentine, R. H. Lacy, and William Dunn, Mr. Huntington's close advisor. This city of the future was to be named "San Marino," after the ranch. It was to be a city of better homes, wide streets, and large lots with provision for garden space. It was to be highly restricted, which meant exclusion of manufacturing plants and inclusion of retail stores only to the extent of supplying local needs.

Mr. Huntington wished to add to the attractiveness of the new subdivision by planting some of his favorite palms, the *Cocos plumosa.* He delegated me to plant these on all tracts subdivided by the Huntington Land and Improvement Company; and in addition to this, to plant from three to five ornamental trees on each of the larger lots.

Up to the time of incorporating the city, everyone who lived in this area was satisfied with the set-up under the existing county government. The need for incor-

[57]

poration, however, was soon evident when reports began to be heard of the intention of neighboring cities to annex to their areas the attractive properties that we were considering as part of the proposed city of San Marino. To forestall unfavorable actions on the part of these nearby cities, therefore, the City of San Marino was incorporated on April 25, 1913. In January of the following year, Mr. Huntington presented to the city the southeast corner lot on Huntington Drive and San Marino Avenue for a city hall site.

Hotel Huntington

It was during the year of 1912 that Mr. Huntington acquired the Wentworth Hotel property which was destined to become the now familiar and widely known Hotel Huntington. The old hotel had been vacant for a number of years and as a result was in a state of neglect. The completion of the structure took place soon after Mr. Huntington's purchase; and he then requested me to landscape the grounds with large specimen plantings to produce immediate effects.

One of the first major moves was the transplanting of twenty-eight large citrus trees: this was a feat in itself. All twenty-eight, save one, grew quite satisfactorily after the transplanting. With the assistance of a crew of fifteen men I was able to revamp the entire grounds before the scheduled opening of the winter season. On opening night our men were used also to help with the parking of the cars of the seemingly endless number of guests.

The firm of Myron Hunt and Elmer Grey, architects, was commissioned to complete the Wentworth Hotel so that it could become the fine hostelry that it has been ever since, and at the completion of this work Mr. Huntington engaged D. M. Linnard, the well-known hotel operator, to manage the newly named Hotel Huntington. It immediately became a success as a winter resort. During the second season we constructed and had ready for the winter opening a nine-hole golf course, and in time the Old Mill was restored to use as a clubhouse, with lockers, showers, and storage space on the lower floor, while the main floor was transformed into a charming clubroom in the then popular Mission style.

Domestic Notes, 1910 = 24

While his house was still under construction, Mr. Huntington discussed in some detail, from time to time, the points he considered essential to the beauty and the comfort of a home. He once said that he believed a home incomplete without the presence of a pet cat. It was not until 1912, however, that he returned from one of his trips to New York with two beautiful angora kittens, one black, the other snow-white: both were tucked away in his drawing-room on the train. By the time he reached California, his severely scratched hands were evidence of a lack of brotherly love between the two male kittens. He had been obliged to separate them frequently during their numerous fights en route.

At that time, the new home was not completely staffed and Mr. Huntington was driven to the necessity of finding a temporary home for the two young pets. One he placed in his son's home in Oak Knoll; the other he requested my wife to care for. We provided bed and board for the coal-black kitten, but it was not as simple a task as one might surmise. Our dog had developed at an early age a definite antipathy toward cats of all shapes and sizes, so the discord between the two may be imagined. Furthermore, the cat was so black that it could never be spotted when it managed to slip outside at night, causing us many moments of concern for its welfare.

The cat and the dog never did overcome their dislike for one another; so the situation was far from one of complete freedom for either. Whenever they chanced to meet they would either fight or stalk by each other, one with ears hanging down, the other with claws stretched out in a menacing manner. Consequently it was with great relief that I learned that Mrs. Foley, the former housekeeper in the Collis P. Huntington home in San Francisco, was to take over the position of housekeeper in the San Marino home and to assume the care of the two cats. Mrs. Foley, however, remained only a short time. In September 1913 Miss Nora Larsen was appointed housekeeper, a position which she held to the utmost satisfaction of the Huntington family until the passing of Mr. Huntington.

Further incident with regard to family pets involved a small Belgian griffon, a dog greatly attached to Mrs. Huntington. This small creature was allowed to take more liberties in the main part of the new home than any human being would have dared to take. It led a pampered and luxurious life until one fateful night, when, as it was being walked by the butler, it made the fatal mistake of springing at a police dog that was accompanying the night watchman on his rounds. The larger dog inflicted an injury to which the small griffon succumbed a few days later. A small coffin was built for the pet and he was buried in Mrs. Huntington's flower garden. She felt very much grieved at the sudden loss, as did the night watchman, who was so upset that he resigned his position.

The Aviary

Mrs. Huntington was very fond of birds and animals, and so it was that on completion of the home, we built for her a large aviary. It extended from the house to the bowling alley (now the tea room). It was divided into twelve sections, with a large dome-like cage in the center that housed twenty-six kinds of parrots and sixty-five other assorted seed-eating birds. Among the latter were two pairs of beautiful blue-crowned Victorian pigeons. Each section was devoted to special collections: for example, one cage contained tumblers, thrushes, crested bulbuls and mynahs; another, parakeets and finches; still another, cockateels and weavers. One cage housed a mixture of fancy pigeons and doves and a fine collection of pheasants.

In order to include water fowls in this collection of birds, it was decided to enlarge the open reservoir, below the lily ponds, to twice its original size and to fill in the center to create an island for nesting. A rustic bridge was built over to one of the banks to make it easily accessible for necessary attention. The water area itself was divided into ten sections by a six-foot-high wire netting which would keep certain birds apart. The island was planted to bamboo and other tall grasses to insure ideal nesting conditions.

The reservoir was then stocked with white and black swans, fancy geese, a few cranes, a stork, and an exceptionally fine collection of ducks. The latter included some handsome mandarins and colorful Mexican wood-ducks. Mr. Huntington spent many leisure hours in this part of the garden, sometimes by himself, but more often in the company of his grandchildren. Together they would sit on the bank and feed the birds.

A spectacular sight on the ranch was that of numbers of peacocks and pheasants allowed to run about at will. Snow-white and blue-and-green peacocks added an astonishing note to the landscape. Among the large collection of other birds were three so valued as to be kept in separate cages. The first was a beautiful white Australian cockatoo with a yellow crest. He was extremely large and spoke a few words. The second was a medium-sized Central American green parrot with a yellow head; he was kept in a regular wire cage in the Huntington home and was by far the best talker of all the parrots. I had purchased him through a dealer in Los Angeles at a reasonable cost. This bird, we found, must have spent some time on board ship: many of his words were typical seaman's expressions, such as "ship ahoy!"

The third bird to be kept in a separate cage was a shiny black Indian mynah with a yellow bill. It was the best talking bird, excelling even the magpies and the parrots. The mynah was kept in a cage in Mrs. Huntington's sitting room and was given considerable attention by the ladies of the household. He was so tame and affectionate that when he was bathed he was taken out of the cage, and never did he attempt to escape. Some might be led to say that he was a smart bird to know enough voluntarily to stay in such an enviable environment. This mynah was the only bird to be allowed to accompany the Huntingtons on their trips to New York. I well remember one occasion when the family was preparing for one of its trips east. I was asked to carry the bird from the limousine to the private car; when I started to do this the bird suddenly shouted, "Where are you going?"

Stables, Dairy, and Poultry Yard

While the Huntington house was under construction we built a modern horse-stable and wagon and equipment sheds of re-enforced concrete. These were built to replace the old barns and shed of the Shorb regime and were in addition to the stables south of Huntington Drive and the one on the El Molino Ranch.

The new stable was large enough to accommodate a dozen draft horses, several saddle horses and a carriage horse. The saddle horses were generally used by Mr. Huntington, Mr. Patton, and Mr. Huntington's secretary, who was then residing at the family mansion. I shall never forget that memorable day when a friend of Mr. Huntington in Kentucky sent him a thoroughbred saddle horse whose express bill amounted to nine hundred dollars! It was a handsome gift.

In order to have a complete estate, it was deemed necessary to add a small dairy to the premises. So I purchased some top-grade Guernsey cows and a thoroughbred Guernsey bull to start our small herd. We then built a modern concrete dairy barn, a silo, and a corral. For pasturage, five acres were planted to alfalfa and four to corn. Finally, to complete the picture, we added to our dairy equipment a modern little milk-house which was furnished with a cream separator and a refrigerator.

The poultry yard was a small institution in itself and seldom housed less than 1,000 fowl at a time. There were sufficient numbers of chickens, turkeys, geese, ducks, guinea-hens, pheasants, and squabs to keep one man busy full time.

The Huntington family was in the habit of using more poultry than any other kind of meat, and the numerous servants in the household shared alike. From March 1916 until July of the same year, an accurate record was maintained of the consumption of poultry and eggs in the Huntington household. The record reads as follows: 554 dozen eggs, 437 chickens, 24 turkeys, 63 ducks, 23 guinea-hens, and 159 squabs.

In 1909 Mr. Huntington was promised the gift of a pair of Oregon black-tail deer by his friend Frank Miller, of the Riverside Mission Inn. We fenced in about three acres that contained a number of large oak trees, near the present library building. It was an ideal location for them, and they multiplied rapidly.

A curious experience taught us that the does became noticeably nervous after the birth of their young. One day while Mrs. Hertrich was observing a new-born fawn, the mother doe suddenly appeared on the spot and without warning raised herself on her hind legs. With her front legs she painfully paddled my wife's back!

Mrs. Huntington's Flower Garden

Mrs. Huntington enjoyed a great variation in garden flowers and cut flowers for the house. Soon she requested that I lay out a small formal garden to be planted to tulips, daffodils, narcissuses, and Spanish and Dutch irises. The following season the garden display provided for her special benefit was composed of some 25,000 tulips and other bulbous plants. It was changed from season to season, using both annuals and perennials, and finally an intermixture of roses was added which eventually became the major part of the cut-flower garden.

Great quantities of cut flowers were used in the house and on the loggia. Arranging, filling, and caring for the many vases and baskets kept a number of the staff very busy. On Sundays and for special occasions I was asked to supervise these arrangements. Due to Mrs. Huntington's impaired eyesight massive displays were requested: she was unable to appreciate a few flowers in a vase, and consequently containers were used which would accommodate from fifty to two hundred flowers. Many a time I have personally arranged as many as two hundred single blooms in one basket. A great number of containers was kept in constant use, mostly the basket-type lined with zinc, one shipment of seventy-five having been received in 1913 from New York.

As a matter of statistical record, the following is an accounting of the cut flowers sent to the Huntington home from their gardens and glass houses for purposes of flower arrangements, during the 1915 season: 950 cattleyas, 150 oncidiums, 400 dendrobiums, 250 phalaenopsids, 100 cypripediums—all members of the orchid family; 3,900 pink and 3,000 white glass-house roses, 2,800 outdoor roses, 3,300 red and 600 white glass-house carnations, 600 cyclamens, 2,400 violets, 600 acacia branches, 1,300 daffodils, 1,000 narcissuses, 200 amaryllises, 2,200 branches of flowering shrubs, 1,000 lilies-of-the-valley, 3,500 irises, 1,800 sweet peas, 700 watsonias, 250 branches of heather, 250 stocks, 2,000 gladioluses, 150 anthuriums; and in addition, numerous flowering plants.

The Flag Pole

The family home was still under construction when the question arose as to where to place a flag pole. If located near the residence, it would have to be very tall or else it would be dwarfed by that large structure. Another item of discussion was whether it should be made of wood or steel.

In the autumn of 1909 Mr. Huntington advised me that he had been promised a very fine pole—an Oregon fir 148 feet tall. It was due to be shipped by a lumber schooner to Redondo Beach; from there I was to transport it to San Marino. I was faced again with a transportation problem that seemed impossible with our limited equipment. But I engaged a stout team of horses and a wagon from our grading contractor, James Montgomery, and with several other men (including Arthur Montgomery), we headed for Redondo.

On the way back with the flag pole, which had to be supported beyond the half mark to keep the end from dragging, we used secondary roads wherever possible to avoid traffic. We made good progress until at one point we reached a right-angle turn in the road. It could not be negotiated without passing over an alfalfa patch in front of a small farmhouse. We tried to locate the owner, who later proved to be a poultry farmer, but at the time he could not be found, though we rang the front door bell and then searched the premises for someone from whom to make inquiry. We finally decided to cross the field without permission. Imagine our surprise on starting across to look up and see the farmer marching out of his house with a shotgun in his hand heading straight for us! He threatened to shoot if we trespassed farther on his property. We quickly assured him of our intention to compensate him for any damage done and to our complete amazement and disbelief, he remarked, "If that's the case, it will be worth a dollar for the privilege."

The trial of transporting the pole was only a part of the difficulties encountered. Reaching San Marino with it, we began excavating for its base. We were obliged to dig a hole sixteen feet deep; then with the aid of a tall guide pole and two guide ropes we were able to lift the pole with block and tackle to an upright position 132 feet above ground level. Mr. Huntington was much pleased with the final results of our efforts, and I personally was very grateful to see the pole firmly anchored in the ground in its concrete base!

Glass Houses

We had built our first glass house in 1908 in order to nurture tropical plants. The collection at first was largely of orchids, of which we made an extensive collection, namely, cattleyas, odontoglossums, ancidiums, lalias, vandals, phalaenopsids, dendrobiums, cypripediums, and a few cymbidiums. Because orchids were Mrs. Huntington's favorite flower, no expense was spared in obtaining a fine, well-balanced collection.

In the year following this first glass-house venture, a second was built, considerably larger than the first. This one was devoted to the culture of rare tropical palms, ferns, anthuriums, and colorful broad-leafed ornamental plants useful for home decoration. The third and last large house was built exclusively for the growing of roses and carnations for winter use. Later six small greenhouses were erected in which to grow winter vegetables.

It was understood that the family would occupy its new home for a total of three to four months the first winter and after that would divide the balance of the year between New York and Paris. World War I upset this schedule and the Huntingtons remained in their San Marino home much longer each winter. Consequently, it became my responsibility to provide the Huntington household with not only winter cut flowers but also dairy products and vegetables. It was to provide the latter, including tomatoes, okra, string beans, cucumbers, melons, and summer squash, that the supplementary smaller greenhouses were built. Although some of these products could have been purchased on the market, it was Mrs. Huntington's wish that the ranch supply everything possible to be used in her kitchen.

Only once did Mr. Huntington make an inquiry of me regarding the cost of producing all these materials. I advised him at that time that melons were costing two dollars and tomatoes a dollar per pound. He commented that his wife was well pleased with the food produced for the kitchen from the premises, and requested that the system of production be continued on the same basis. In addition, we soon established mushroom beds in the basement of the garage building.

Canyon Storm Drain

In 1907 Mr. Huntington acquired from his neighbor, George S. Patton, an additional tract of land which included a very beautiful oak-studded canyon. Through this we were able to construct a winding road as a new approach to the gateway leading to Pasadena, the termination point being Rosalind Road.

This canyon was an outlet for storm water draining as far north as San Pasqual Street. In the early days before this section had been built upon and improved, the hay and grain pastures had absorbed most of the rains and the canyon had taken care of the excess water. But as soon as improvements were made and the open fields were no longer there, the surplus water increased to the extent of lowering the floor of the waterway every winter.

We first installed some check dams, but the increased volume of water, we found, could only be controlled by building a storm drain the entire length of the canyon, a matter of 4,440 feet. Since tentative bids for the job seemed excessively high, I purchased a small concrete mixer and with my own crew installed the necessary storm drain. The planting of native shrubs and ferns, plus the installation of ornamental guard rails, added to the improvements.

The Roof Garden

To improve the outlook from Mrs. Huntington's dressing room through the French doors opening onto the roof of the loggia, I installed at one time a small roof garden, using ornamental lattice work to make a pergola with several arches. We placed about a dozen bay trees and acacias, established in large tubs or boxes, on this roof, improving the view from the French windows, as well as eliminating considerable glare from the roof top into the room. It also provided, of course, a pleasant variation of color during the seasons, as the flowering trees came into bloom.

The Turtle Pond

During the second season the family spent in California Mrs. Huntington informed me that she was to be the recipient of approximately one hundred diamond-back terrapins from the South. The question naturally arose as to where to place them. The lily ponds were out of the question, as well as the pond in the Japanese garden, because these had cement bottoms and the sides were not fenced.

To meet this unanticipated acquisition we were obliged to excavate a special pond for the turtles, north of the aviary, which we enclosed with a wire fence. Sand banks had to be provided where the turtles could deposit and hatch their eggs. Surprisingly enough they liked their new home when they became settled and increased in numbers sufficiently to replace those which were caught to be used in the Huntington kitchen. Some of these specimens may still be found in the lily ponds, to which they were transplanted after the turtle pond was abandoned.

Mrs. Huntington's formal flower garden

FLAG POLE, *flanked by Australian Kauri Pine, with rose pergola and aviary in background*

PART OF CYCAD COLLECTION *in the rockery*

ENCEPHALARTOS ALTENSTEINII

Africa (seed-bearing cone)

CYCAS REVOLUTA

Asia (seed-bearing cone)

FRUITING SPECIMENS OF CYCADS, *a family of plants descendant of the earliest plant life recorded in fossil form. They have a wide distribution, each one indigenous to a different continent.*

MACROZAMIA DENISONII

Australia (pollen-bearing cone)

DION EDULE

North America (pollen-bearing cone)

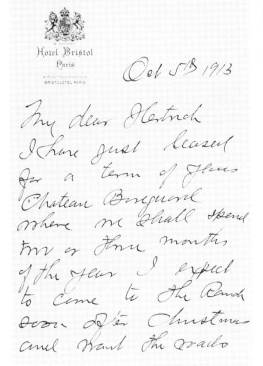

Hotel Bristol
Paris

Oct 5th 1913

My dear Hertrich
I have just leased
for a term of years
Chateau Beauregard
where we shall spend
two or three months
of the year I expect
to come to the Ranch
soon after Christmas
and want the roads

**A LETTER FROM
MR. HUNTINGTON**

all in nice condition when I
arrive and also have the driving
horses well groomed when I get
there If you have no turkeys on
the place you had better purchase
some would like to get white
ones if you can at any rate
get good ones I hear that Genl
Hewlett has given up Howards place
perhaps you can buy his
birds now at a fair price
I am very glad you got the
Bradbury plants give me a list of
what you got from him send it
to New York as I sail from
here the 19th and will reach
New York about the 25th my
address there will be 2 East 57 St
I tell you Hertrich I have seen no
place as nice as the ranch
with kindest regards Yours truly
H E Huntington

CHATEAU BEAUREGARD *in France, where*
the Huntingtons spent a few summers

JAPANESE GARDEN *after completion of landscaping, 1913*

TORII GATE *at south entrance to Japanese garden, the timbers for which were shipped from Alaska to form the supports for the carved front of the totem poles in the Indian Village in Los Angeles*

BELL TOWER AND TEMPLE BELL *in Japanese garden. The tower was erected by a Japanese workman without use of nails*

PINK-FLOWERED WISTERIA *In front of Japanese tea house*

The Rockery

When the exterior of the Huntington home was completed we began to landscape the gardens adjacent to it. Mr. Huntington was most anxious for us to complete the planned rockery early in this program: it was to be located to the north of the loggia. The site lent itself admirably to certain types of exotic plants requiring semishade and protection against frosts. To enhance the setting of these semitropical plants, I searched the country over for a suitable type of porous rock.

Finally, near Santa Cruz, I found the desired product. It was a soft tufa stone, light in weight and soft enough to be cut with a cross-cut saw. We loaded two large open steel freight cars to capacity with it and sent them on to their destination—the spur track terminal in San Marino. At first, of course, their barren aspect made an artificial effect, but soon they became attractively weatherbeaten and appropriately overgrown with vegetation.

As soon as this tufa stone was placed we began to plant out ferns, begonias, cyclamens, cinerarias, large specimens of cycads, and then finished the project with some of the hardy, but as yet untried, orchids. The latter included the coelogynes, odontoglossums, lalias, ancidiums, cypripediums, and a few cymbidiums and epidendrums. This was the first time cymbidiums had been planted out of doors in Southern California; since then they have become favorite garden specimens with amateurs and professionals alike.

The Cycad Collection

One of the most difficult groups of plants to assemble was that of the cycads. Chiefly because of their rarity and slow growth, they were not profitable for nurseries to handle; but they could be found occasionally in private collections or in botanical gardens.

This particular group of plants is indigenous to many parts of the globe: they are decorative specimens for conservatories and thrive under such conditions in most regions. In subtropical countries they grow out of doors. In Mexico I found the genera *dioon,* the fern-like *zamia,* and the *ceratozamia,* all natives of that country, and I was able to bring back some very good specimens of all of them.

I began to locate a few isolated specimens of this group of plants, occasionally in horticultural establishments of the eastern United States, particularly at W. A. Manda's in South Orange, New Jersey. Later on, I realized that the best sources for fine specimens were Sanders and Sons of London, England, and Brugg's in Belgium.

About this time, two competing collectors of cycads, Arthur Letts of Hollywood and Louis Bradbury of Duarte, were also scouring the same fields for desirable specimens. Such combined activity in this limited field brought about a noticeable shortage in this type of plant. It was perhaps only human that I should be envious of Mr. Bradbury's collection, not only of his cycads, but of his other rare and tropical as well as subtropical plants; he had a distinct advantage over me because during his spare time he had traveled to Europe and the Orient and had in many instances selected specimens on the spot. I visited his grounds occasionally and we would exchange friendly opinions about the various rare items that he possessed.

I had been keeping in touch with Fred Sanders of London by correspondence and learned at one time that he contemplated a trip to the United States. He had advised me that he planned to pay me a visit in order to show me photographs of some fine specimens of African cycads which he had recently acquired from a large estate in Europe. Arriving in Los Angeles, he stopped at the Hotel Alexandria and quite by chance met Mr. Bradbury in the lobby shortly after his arrival. Bradbury naturally inquired about the purpose of his long trip, and Sanders showed the photographs of the plants: promptly Bradbury purchased them. The next day at the time of our appointed visit I learned to my dismay of my rival collector's good fortune. But I was assured first choice of the next available material.

In September 1913 Frank Nelson, who was Mr. Bradbury's superintendent, advised me that his employer intended to dismantle his glass houses and was planning to sell his rare tropical and subtropical collection, including the cycads, at a very reasonable figure. I immediately cabled this information to Mr. Huntington, at that time in Paris, and he authorized me to use my own judgment in the matter.

That very afternoon I drove to Bradbury's, leaving two wagons and a half dozen men about a block from the residence. After concluding the deal, which was satisfactory, I signaled for the men to come up with the wagons. We then loaded the most valuable plants into the wagons and started for San Marino Ranch. I deemed this precaution necessary to guard against Mr. Bradbury's changing his mind overnight.

In Search of Rare Plants

It was about 1912 that I went east on a trip in search of rare plants, and to serve as one of the judges at the First International Flower Show in New York. Mr. Huntington was also in town and together we visited the show, taking that opportunity to select plants for his California estate. The second day we again visited the show, accompanied this time by Mrs. C. P. Huntington: this was the first time I had met this lady, who later became Mrs. Henry E. Huntington. He was delighted to be able to show her the plants that we had purchased the day before, as well as others that we intended to purchase for the San Marino Ranch.

It was on this same trip that I met Baron Natili, a life-long friend of the family, at the Metropolitan Club, where Mr. Huntington was staying. The baron was a subsequent guest at San Marino Ranch, at least two seasons, as I remember. While at the club Mr. Huntington, on a later occasion, called to my attention a seemingly endless number of books stacked in every possible place, even under his bed. This was only a portion of the now-famed rare-book collection which at that time he was already steadily increasing. This particular lot was waiting to be shipped by express, a few cases at a time, to the ranch, where they were to be stored in a safe place, always arriving via Wells Fargo Express "dead head" under Mr. Huntington's franking privilege.

Plans For a Ranch of My Own

After a number of years' experience at the ranch, I seriously considered acquiring a small acreage of my own to plant to either citrus or avocado trees or a combination of both. When I finally found the location I thought a good purchase prospect, I talked over the plans with Mr. Huntington. He was simply astonished that I'd ever entertained a thought of purchasing ranch property for myself, explaining his astonishment by saying that he felt I had plenty of ground to oversee at that time, and furthermore that I would have the acreage of San Marino Ranch "to play with" as long as I lived. It was obvious that he was not pleased with my proposed plan: perhaps he believed that property of my own might well cause me to divert necessary time and energy from his estate. He advised me not to consider the matter further, but instead to give thought to another type of investment. He also stressed to the key-men of his staff of workers that they must consistently save a percentage of their earnings, and he made a definite point of finding out how these personal finances were being handled. Many times he mentioned to me that his uncle, Collis P. Huntington, would not retain a man in any responsible position if he did not save a part of his earnings.

Mr. Huntington held an unfaltering love for his own ranch, as he called the estate, and he so expressed himself frequently. On his first trip to Europe, I remember, which occurred in 1913, he visited many outstanding gardens, but invariably he would write at the end of his letters after mentioning them, "Hertrich, I still believe I like the ranch the best."

He was a true lover of nature and largely because of that disliked formality in the garden plan: he often stated as much to me and asked me to refrain from formality wherever possible. His wife did not share his feeling, but agreed that with the exception of a small, formal, cut-flower garden the ranch should be free of formal plantings.

The Japanese Garden

During the summer of 1912 Mr. Huntington suggested that I prepare a plan to improve the small canyon to the west of the rose garden. Mr. Shorb, the former owner, had installed a dam across the south end and had used it as a reservoir. It appeared that the dam could be leveled and thus an unsightly spot could be transformed into an attractive garden, possibly a Japanese garden. I made this suggestion to Mr. Huntington. The idea was acceptable, but Mr. Huntington's chief concern was the time element. I estimated that it would take six months to complete the project properly but he wanted it ready sooner, so that it would all be in perfect order that following winter, when his family planned to occupy the new home.

We immediately went to work with the bare possibility in mind that it would be sufficiently finished in time to be a source of satisfaction to the family. We leveled off the dam, installed the rockery and waterfall, excavated for the ponds, whose walls and bottoms we lined with concrete, and finally, we installed bridges, walks, and steps.

While the above work was progressing I searched throughout every nursery in California for Oriental plants that we needed so desperately to complete the plan. As a last resort I approached the owner of a commercial Japanese tea garden which was located on the northeast corner of Fair Oaks Avenue and California Streets in Pasadena, hoping he would allow me to purchase some of his large specimen plants. Very politely he informed me, however, that none of the plants was available for sale.

[78]

Continuing the conversation, I learned that the tea garden had proved to be a financial failure, and that he really was most anxious to sell the entire property and all of the ornaments and fixtures. I conveyed this important piece of information to Mr. Huntington, who promptly ordered the property and all it contained to be bought immediately.

Shortly after completing this business transaction four crews of men set to work in earnest. One group boxed and balled the plants to be moved, while another dismantled the buildings, bridges, and garden shelters. A third crew used three teams of horses and wagons to transport this material to the ranch; while a fourth worked to plant the material as fast as the trees and shrubs were delivered. By this "streamlined" method, the Japanese garden was completed in record time. Since we were able to use large enough plants to produce an effect of a long-established garden, Mr. Huntington's wish was fulfilled in having the canyon area a spot of beauty when the family arrived to occupy its new home.

Not long after the establishment of this garden, we received a shipment from the Orient which included Japanese lanterns, miniature pagodas, and stone idols which were set out in appropriate spots. Still later we secured the services of a Japanese craftsman who designed and constructed the Full-Moon bridge, and at a later date, the ornate enclosure for the temple bell, a late acquisition. The bell tower was erected by this workman without the use of nails.

At the south entrance to this Oriental garden the Torii gate was erected, lending a touch of "local color" to the landscape. It was constructed from timbers shipped from Alaska and originally received at the Indian Village, which was then located adjacent to Lincoln Park. These timbers, almost three feet in diameter, were once used as supports for totem poles, first in Alaska, then in the Village in Los Angeles. Antonio Apache was responsible for the establishing of the Indian Village, which was financially supported by Mr. Huntington and several others, including, as I remember, William G. Kerckhoff. It was Antonio who made the arrangement to ship the totem poles to Los Angeles about 1906. Subsequently the Village was abandoned and at that time I was able to secure the timbers to use in the landscaping plan of the Japanese garden, ideal material for the Torii gate.

Proper maintenance of this garden could not be continued in the necessary details during future years, due to restricted budgets and the inability to procure suitable personnel. At the time the garden was completed, a Japanese family, including a father, mother, and three children, were hired to live in the two-story Japanese house that had been built on the far slope of the canyon, and to care for the garden. An Oriental atmosphere was thus produced and was further enhanced on occasion by the family's custom of dressing up in Japanese costume for special holidays. But so ideal a situation, both from the aesthetic point of view and the practical standpoint, could not be carried out for more than a few years. The house since has been abandoned as living quarters. Many of the plants of the surrounding garden have grown out of all proportion to the original intention, and no longer fit into the scale designed for them.

Move Into the New Residence

Many delays, largely unforeseen, postponed the Huntington family's occupancy of its new home. The original schedule set the date in 1911, but final completion of all work, plus change of family plans, combined to push the date up to January 1914.

As early as 1911, however, we began to install some of the household equipment and also to bring in some of the art objects. The latter was done under Mr. Huntington's personal guidance. I assisted him, with the aid of three or four men, depending upon the tasks involved, size and weight of materials to be moved, etc. All of the delicate material and fragile pieces, such as crystal-ware, porcelains, marble statues, bronzes, I unpacked myself, assisted by only one man. This experience proved to be of considerable value to me, for later I was obliged to repack some of these articles for reshipment.

After moving quantities of such valuable statuary, paintings, and art objects, we felt we were becoming experts. Through 1912 and up to the time the family moved into the residence in 1914, shipments continued to come in. Often during these years, when Mr. Huntington was in California living at the Jonathan Club, I would telephone him about the arrival of an important shipment, since he so palpably enjoyed being present when the materials were being unpacked.

An interesting sidelight on Mr. Huntington's character and convictions occurred one time when he was seated near the kitchen entrance watching us unpack two boxes of goods. He began to pick up all the better pieces of paper, folding them neatly; then he selected the longer pieces of string, rolled them into small coils, and placed them with the salvaged paper. After the men had left for lunch, I casually mentioned to Mr. Huntington that he was keeping busy, to which he replied, "Yes, Hertrich, and it's not so much the value of the paper and string as the example it sets for the men; to impress on them the fact that nothing is too small or too insignificant to save."

This recalls also another incident which was related to me after it had occurred, illustrating the same philosophy. One evening when Mr. and Mrs. Huntington were playing cards, Mr. Huntington noticed a light burning unnecessarily; he left the game, walked down the hall, and switched off the light. On his return, Mrs. Huntington said, "Edward, I simply can't understand why you walk to the end of that long hall to save a few pennies, when the next minute you'll turn around and pay as much as ten thousand dollars for an old book." He replied, "My dear, if I did not save the pennies, I couldn't buy the ten-thousand-dollar book."

At every opportunity Mr. Huntington let it be known that saving is a good habit to acquire and that waste of any kind was in his opinion inexcusable. I remember one day while we were riding up in an elevator together to his office in the Pacific Electric Building, he remarked to me, "Hertrich, that is a nice suit you are wearing; is it new?" I replied, "No. I had it made to order about two years ago." To prove my statement, I exposed the tailor's label on the inside of the coat pocket. He laughed and said, "I go you one better. Mine was made over three years ago!" And he likewise showed me the tailor's label inside his pocket.

Of the garden ornaments that arrived even after the home was finally completed, most came in car lots. One consignment alone contained several of the smaller fountains, one large marble seat that weighed over three tons, some statuary and numerous vases. On the whole, most of the items arrived in good condition.

Perhaps the most difficult item to install was the large stone fountain which was placed at the end of the North Vista. It was shipped in 48 boxes, filled an entire railroad car, and carried a total weight of 42 tons, exclusive of the basin. The basin we designed and constructed with the help of our own staff—a practice we followed with regard to the basins of all other fountains installed on the premises. The chief difficulty we encountered in assembling the large fountain was that the consignors had neglected to mark the pieces at the time of dismantling. Naturally many of the pieces looked somewhat alike but did not fit together. This necessitated our handling many of the heavy sections time and time again until the right one was found.

The fountain located in front of the library building presented no difficulties whatever in assembling, nor did the stone temple with the wrought-iron grilled dome. The small marble temple placed along the west side of the North Vista was equally simple to install. Mr. Huntington acquired most of these items at random, and selected a place for them after they arrived at the ranch. He enjoyed walking about the grounds looking for the proper place to set a vase, statue, or fountain. Often I would accompany him, carrying a few stakes that could be placed wherever he decided to locate a particular piece. Some of the items I moved once, twice, or even more; but others seemed ideally situated at the first placement. A great deal of time was devoted to finding a suitable position for the marble fountain in the rockery. Another entire afternoon was given to selecting a place for Frederick MacMonnies' "Bacchante," a bronze statuette. Mr. Huntington, the sculptor, and I, with the aid of two laborers, pulled this statuette around with us while we were selecting the suitable place for it: an open exposure facing south. We finally set it under some trees on top of the marble fountain in the rockery, facing north!

Mr. Huntington was constantly improving not only his collection of paintings, but also the collection of ornaments such as vases for both inside and outside: like the paintings they were often installed tentatively until more suitable items could be procured. For example, the vases on the balustrade along the south terrace were placed and replaced three times. The first set of twenty-five was made to order by W. Bauman of Los Angeles, after a pattern cast from white cement and white quartz sand. A few years later Mr. Huntington purchased a set of white marble vases to replace the cement ones; and the vases were again changed during subsequent years as he bought a few at a time of a more interesting type of vase made of marble and stone. A closely similar procedure was followed with the vases placed on the balcony and roof balustrade: the last selection was a set of lead vases. The latter required special treatment during the summer of 1938: although giving the appearance of being substantial, these top-heavy ornate pieces were vulnerable to the reflected heat of the house walls and the tiled floor of the balcony in this southern exposure. One of the vases, all of which began to sag noticeably, collapsed completely, falling to the terrace below, a total wreck. As a result, the remaining pieces were lined with cement on the inside as a precaution against future damage or loss.

Other garden ornaments, over a period of years, have shown signs of deterioration due to exposure to the Southern California climate. Expansion and contraction caused by the extreme changes of temperature between day- and night-time at certain seasons resulted, in some instances, in many fine, hair-thin cracks, chiefly in stone and marble pieces which had been previously repaired with iron dowels. Moisture crept in, causing the iron dowels to rust and expand enough to push apart some of the mended pieces. All of the iron dowels had to be replaced eventually with bronze or brass; and as an added precaution, thorough application of transparent paraffin-base waterproofing was made, a procedure it was necessary to repeat every few years.

Over the period of several years when I was obliged to move the house and ground ornaments to the spots considered most suitable by Mr. Huntington, my crew of men who helped in this exacting work deserved much credit. They took considerable pride in handling successfully the delicate items. Some of the household pieces had highly polished surfaces to be protected; some of the larger pictures to be hung had heavy but extremely brittle frames. But all necessary operations were performed remarkably well and with a minimum of breakage. Our equipment and ingenuity were strained almost to the limit in placing some of the heavier statuary. For example, the four stone statues which once were at the Hofburg, the Hapsburg Imperial Palace in Vienna, and which came to us by an all-water route, delivered at San Pedro, were excessively heavy. Another unwieldy group was that composed of the four large bronze figures now located in front of the library building.

In great measure the success we had in handling all this material—installing, dismantling, moving, and reinstalling—was due to the full co-operation of the aforementioned crew: John Gombotz, who was in charge of the maintenance of the residence and the library for many years; George Chaplin, who was in charge of the maintenance of the pumps and general water system; Otto Veit, our mason and cement finisher; and Paul Kley, the house carpenter. With the exception of John Gombotz, now deceased, all of these men are still employed by the institution.

As for the modern furniture which was to accommodate the needs of the family as occupants of the residence, shipments came in from Grand Rapids in two freight cars. Most of this, which again involved unpacking and carrying into the living quarters on the second floor, was handled by the same crew of men. Among some of Mr. Huntington's possessions from former years was a beautiful cherry-wood bookcase built in three sections, with carved panels. We moved this particular piece from one room to another, never finding a suitable place for it. Finally Mr. Huntington said, "Hertrich, if you can find room in your home for this bookcase, I shall make a present of it to you." Some time later his son Howard told me that this particular bookcase was the first one his father had owned, and that that was doubtless his sole reason for trying to find an appropriate spot for it in his new home.

Automobiles

When I first arrived in San Marino, Mr. Huntington owned a pair of carriage horses. These were later supplanted by his first automobile, a Stevens-Duryea which was kept in a Los Angeles garage. Mr. Huntington's varied interests combined to keep him away from Los Angeles a good part of the time, so at first a chauffeur was hired on a temporary basis. This arrangement proved unsatisfactory because good reliable men desired permanent positions. This situation was remedied later when the new garage and living quarters for a chauffeur were constructed on the ranch. We then employed a full-time chauffeur-mechanic.

The first automobiles housed in the ranch garage were two American Morris cars, one a limousine weighing 5,600 pounds, the other a touring car weighing 4,800 pounds. These were the largest and heaviest cars ever possessed by Mr. Huntington. They were later replaced by two Loziers, again a limousine and a touring car, both of which were in constant service until 1919 when Mr. Huntington purchased three Locomobiles: a limousine, a touring car, and a town car. Later he acquired a second Locomobile limousine.

For service we first used a 1911 Cadillac, then an Oldsmobile and a motorcycle with a side-car. By this time my work and general responsibility had expanded to the point where I was obliged to use an automobile to do efficient work. At the beginning, I used the Cadillac part time; then an Abbot-Detroit which I drove some 55,000 miles; three Oldsmobiles driven a minimum of 80,000 miles each; a Chrysler that covered 81,000 miles; and finally, a Hupmobile with a record of 93,000 miles.

Mr. Huntington owned also an electric-powered automobile which he learned to operate himself. He used this car primarily to take leisurely drives about the estate, frequently accompanied by Mrs. Huntington. At intervals he would venture outside to various parts of San Marino and the Oak Knoll district of Pasadena, observing the improvements under way on his property and that belonging to his neighbors.

Sundry Buildings

It was about the time that the foundation work for the new home was started in 1909 that Mr. Huntington expressed anxiety to have a substantial garage built to house his automobiles, which up to that time had been kept in a shed. In time such a garage was built—of re-enforced concrete with tile- and brick-filled wall. This building was equipped with a modern repair shop and underground storage for gasoline, distillate and oils; and in addition it provided living quarters for a married couple and rooms for two single men.

A small building of construction similar to that of the garage was built a bit later to provide office space for Mr. Huntington and myself. It also later accommodated Gilbert L. Brown, bookkeeper and subsequently auditor. This was about two hundred yards east of the residence. It proved to be inadequate in size, so as soon as the residence was completed, Mr. Huntington gave up his quarters there and the small library room in his home served him as an office.

Soon after the family took up residence in January 1914 it became very evident that additional servants' quarters were needed. The following season while the family was away from San Marino, we built four more rooms for the women servants in the spacious attic of the home, and also a small building to the north of the residence to be used for recreational purposes by the servants. To this we later added, as well, two rooms for additional male servants. The bedrooms installed in the attic did not prove very convenient so were later abandoned as such, in favor of quarters in a new cottage erected north of the recreation cottage, containing six bedrooms with bath facilities, a more satisfactory arrangement in every way.

The last of the various buildings put up on the premises was designated for family recreation: it contained the little-used billiard room and the bowling alley.

Personnel

During my forty-two-year tenure as superintendent of the San Marino Ranch I was, of course, associated with all types of personnel, and I learned their abilities, their limitations, their likes and dislikes. I found that, although the workers included all nationalities, some division of work was desirable to make for the best efficiency. For instance the Western Europeans made the best household employees, and among them also were to be found the few skilled artisans who were needed. The majority of unskilled laborers were Mexicans, with the exception of one Chinese and one Japanese. Automotive mechanics were American boys.

Capable household help was difficult to obtain because the Huntington home was located so far from city regions, as well as some little walking distance from the local railway station. For the most part, however, we were fortunate in our selection of employees in this department; harmony and loyalty were usually evident. Only once was a sudden discharge necessary.

Employees hired to care for the grounds changed from time to time, as the type of work in progress took on different character and as living quarters were available. In the earliest days, Mexican labor only was to be had. Mexicans proved satisfactory ranch workers so long as they could work in groups under the supervision of a capable foreman. Two or three of the Mexican boys became expert in the handling of the large streams of irrigating water, wasting the least amount of water possible. When housing accommodations were provided very little difficulty was experienced in procuring skilled laborers of all sorts: American, European, Oriental, etc. Group work was arranged so as to maintain working harmony and to produce as efficient work as possible.

During World War I, certain jealous and prejudiced individuals accused me of maintaining a large number of ex-German soldiers on the Huntington payroll. I referred the accusation to the proper authorities. As a result of their investigations, it was found that the criticism was not justified, and Mr. Huntington instructed me to carry on as before in developing the necessary personnel to care for his properties.

The Life of a Superintendent

It was Mr. Huntington's urgent wish that everything should be done to make Mrs. Huntington's brief periods in her California home comfortable and fraught with minimum inconvenience. As a consequence, I was on twenty-four-hour call at all times during the months the family spent in the California ranch residence. We were all aware of Mrs. Huntington's express preference for living in New York and in Paris, also of Mr. Huntington's desire to make her visits to California something to be remembered with pleasure.

Since the Huntington home was then located in a section considered as "the country," it may perhaps be easily understood how mishaps could occur which were very difficult to rectify immediately. The structure was new and of tremendous proportions for private living; many adjustments and improvements were necessary in the process of becoming "settled." I remember a few experiences vividly, especially during the winter rainstorms, of which some were such that I barely escaped with my life.

During 1914, which was the first season the family spent the winter as residents of the ranch home, the house maintenance man telephoned me on one occasion to advise me that one of the large furnaces equipped with a new type of gas burner was not functioning properly. I went to investigate the situation. As I approached close enough to determine the reason for the poor performance of the equipment, an accumulation of gas exploded which hurled me against a wall fifteen feet away, and burned off much of the skin on my face and hands. Needless to say, very shortly after this narrow escape from blindness or possible death, the gas burners were discarded and replaced by wood and coal furnaces.

At another time, the housekeeper frantically telephoned me one evening, claiming that my immediate presence was needed. It appeared that water was dripping through the ceiling of Mrs. Huntington's dressing-room and one of the bedrooms. A check-up proved that a faulty water pipe in the attic was the cause of the trouble. But already one of the valuable paintings had absorbed enough moisture to cause it to appear like a corrugated washboard. Some of the drapes also had become slightly discolored from the dripping water. The chief problem, however, centered in the closets of Mrs. Huntington's dressing-room: water had begun to seep in. As was customary, all of the closet doors were locked and only Mrs. Huntington knew the whereabouts of the keys. Securing the services of a locksmith in time to avoid serious damage to the delicate laces, fabrics, shawls, and clothing so carefully locked away was an impossibility. We therefore were forced to the decision of breaking the hinges on all the closet doors. The housekeeper removed the affected pieces, carefully dried and ironed them, and finally restored them to their proper places. The hinges of the doors were then properly repaired, screwed back on, the chipped paint retouched; and as far as I know Mrs. Huntington was never cognizant of the unfortunate happening, although I told Mr. Huntington about it when he returned the next winter.

During another rainy winter I was called again to the residence about midnight to investigate another leak. This proved to be caused by a faulty drain. The trouble this time was in the wall behind a valuable tapestry. The indoor portion of the job that confronted us was comparatively simple after the tapestry had been removed; but the next step obliged me to climb up onto the roof to locate the inlet to the drain so that further leakage and entrance of water into the house could be prevented. The tracing of the trouble was not as difficult as it might have been had I not been so thoroughly familiar with the numerous inlets. The task was completed in record time in this instance.

In 1916, one morning about two A.M. an emergency call came during a very heavy rainstorm. The Huntington residence and its occupants were in distress. Driving over there I had the unhappy experience of steering my car onto the soft shoulder of the road, stalling the car, as I tried to avoid a particularly swift stream of gushing water. So I was obliged to walk the remaining distance, and I arrived at the residence to find everyone in a state of extreme agitation and excitement. Mr. Huntington, clad only in a nightshirt, and with broom in hand, was attempting to sweep the rapidly accumulating water out through the double doors leading to the balcony. Servants with buckets and towels were futilely trying to keep the water from streaming down the staircase and entering the second floor sitting-room. Again I made my way to the roof where I noted that the gutters were inadequate to carry away the deluge of rain waters. The overflow had fallen to the balcony in such quantities as to force its way into the upper hall whence it flowed down the steps and into the sitting-room.

All we could do that night was to stuff toweling into all the openings to keep out additional water. The following morning, the storm still continuing, we provided emergency drainage by cutting openings through the base rail of the balcony balustrade.

It was in this same year of 1916, which was notable for excessively heavy rains, that a call came to me to open the emergency valves at Wilson Lake, which had begun to overflow into Old Mill Road. Accompanied by a helper, I drove up the road as far as I could; then the car stalled and we walked the rest of the way to the lake. By that time the heavy flow of storm water from Kewen Canyon had caused the water to rise in the newly formed lake to such an extent that I realized it had submerged my stalled car. It was not until the following morning that the water receded sufficiently to allow the car to be towed home.

One stormy Sunday evening while Mr. Huntington was entertaining a dozen guests at dinner all lights went out without warning, leaving the house in total darkness. Candles were used and I was summoned to find the cause of the interruption of electric service. Subsequent search disclosed that a tree had been blown over, breaking one of the wires. Such incidents were particularly embarrassing and annoying to Mrs. Huntington. When the Huntington residence was being built it was planned that the supply of electricity was to come through the Pacific Light and Power Company, which was a company largely owned by Mr. Huntington and Mr. Kerckhoff. Mrs. Huntington several times expressed the opinion that it was very strange for such poor service to come from a company practically owned by her husband—generally adding that such inconveniences never happened in New York!

A source of great concern about this time was Mr. Huntington's safety during the Los Angeles Railway strike. Mrs. Huntington was gravely distressed—just one of the more serious troubles that seemed to beset her during California sojourns. She requested me to accompany Mr. Huntington to and from his office, virtually acting as his bodyguard. This was one of the several unusual phases of my job as superintendent of Mr. Huntington's interests and property in San Marino.

Some Pleasanter Phases

From the above accounts it should not be felt that the major part of my experiences as Mr. Huntington's superintendent were calamitous and distressing. I thoroughly enjoyed the pleasant environment in which I lived and worked. The knowledge that Mr. Huntington thoroughly approved of and appreciated my efforts also afforded me a great deal of satisfaction. I actually have felt great pride in having been accorded the privilege of initiating the successful foundation of the now famous Huntington Botanical Gardens. But I remember too that the project has been one the success of which has depended upon hard work, ingenuity and infinite patience throughout the years.

A certain number of "extra-curricular" activities have also been a part of my interesting life in these surroundings. Aside from supervising and constantly seeking methods to improve the gardens and ranch properties, I have found time to serve on agricultural and horticultural committees in San Marino, in nearby communities, and occasionally in other parts of the country. I have been credited with planting the first avocado orchard in Southern California. This was a project that entailed considerable time in obtaining the proper information pertaining to best varieties of avocado trees and their culture, and further time in helping to spread this information as a member of the Avocado Growers Variety Committee.

I have willingly endeavored to act to the best of my ability as a source of advisory information for professional and amateur horticultural organizations, lecturing on various subjects and eagerly sharing where I could the results of the extensive experience my profession has given me. The lectures have been a chore, however, and I have kept them to a minimum. Another task with a modicum of the tedious about it has been that of flower judging, which I have done since 1905 all across the country as far east as New York.

Shortly after the San Marino School District was established I was appointed to that Board, serving out the term of a member whom I replaced, Mrs. Clare A. Pattie, and being elected for another term. In 1922 I served as a member of the San Marino City Council during the temporary absence of George S. Patton, who was traveling extensively in Europe at the time. A year later I was again appointed to the same Board to fill another vacancy and served in that capacity until my resignation twenty-three years later in the autumn of 1945.

During my tenure of office as a member of the Council I also served as Chairman of the Park Commission, designing and supervising the development of Lacy Park. Police and fire commissioner officerships were an added part of the community duties that were undertaken and carried until the time I sent in my resignations. These duties afforded many an interesting contact and a welcome variation in the activities connected with my profession.

Because of the pressure of work and endless responsibilities I was unable to take a vacation from 1920 until after 1927, the year of Mr. Huntington's death, a full year being required after that event to convert the private estate into a public institution. So it was during the summer of 1928 that plans were completed to enable Mrs. Hertrich and myself to take a trip which proved to be a combination business and pleasure trip to Europe. We visited many of the famed museums and art galleries for the purpose of comparing their operation with that of the Huntington properties. Of course, I was also deeply interested in the European botanical and horticultural institutions whence I hoped to acquire additional rare plant material. While in Central Europe I lectured in Munich before the Horticultural Society there and again in Vienna, on the subject of the Huntington Botanical Gardens, illustrating the talks with natural-color slides.

In 1936 at the personal invitation of the Viscountess Byng, president at that time of England's Alpine Garden Society, I went to England to lecture on the rock gardens of California. The occasion was the conference of this Society, held in the Hall of the Royal Horticultural Society of London. I again used color slides to illustrate this lecture. From there my wife and I departed once more for the Continent to continue my everlasting search for new plant material.

The highlight of the Alpine Garden conference was a dinner given by Lord and Lady Aberconway at their London town house. A large group of local and foreign horticulturists attended, and my wife enjoyed immensely being seated next to the Honorable David Bowes-Lyon (brother of Queen Elizabeth) who evinced much interest in the conversation about the English paintings housed in the Huntington Art Gallery at San Marino. We also enjoyed a delightful weekend stay at the country home of Lady Byng in Sussex.

GREEK TEMPLE, *placed at entrance to rose garden*

"LITTLE LADY FROM THE SEA," *bronze by Janet Scudder*

THE NORTH VISTA, *looking toward the Sierra Madre Mountains*

DETAIL OF LARGE FOUNTAIN OF ISTRIA STONE, *North Vista, facing south*

SOUTH TERRACE
OF RESIDENCE

Showing vases on balustrade

Above: Original vases, cast from concrete, about 1911

Right: Third and final set of stone and marble urns, about 1922

THE LOGGIA *during the family's occupancy of the house*

FAMILY
CROQUET
COURT

MR. HUNTINGTON *enjoying the North Vista*

MR. HUNTINGTON *on the path between residence and office.*
Site of the present library building

"BACCHANTE," *bronze, by Frederick MacMonnies*

Deed of Trust

Necessity for changing boundary lines, entrances, and generally altering various aspects of the ranch came with Mr. Huntington's decision in 1919 to execute a deed of trust setting aside 200 acres of ground and all its appurtenances as part of an institution to be known as the Henry E. Huntington Library and Art Gallery. This was effected on August 30, 1919.

Several considerations determined the acreage thus allocated: it had been our intention at the beginning of the vast planting program twelve years prior to this time, and our continued effort ever since, to maintain a living collection of exotic plants. After various conferences with Mr. Huntington it was decided that 200 acres would be enough land for the establishment of such a botanic garden.

Adjustment of the boundary lines was the first step. The 200 acres set aside as a permanent grant formed, in conjunction with the home and the library building, the heart of the San Marino Ranch. New boundary lines had to be determined on all sides, leaving the balance of the ranch available for homesite subdivision. The southern line was moved north to a new street, Euston Road. Along the eastern side, Oxford Road was cut through; and the northern boundary was designated as Orlando Road. A problem then arose over a subdivision of very short hillside lots that were to face a new street extending through the bottom of Mission Canyon. The matter was finally adjusted to everyone's satisfaction when the property owners to the west acquired the short lots as extensions to their property. The idea of a street through the canyon was abandoned. The new boundary line was established along the center line of the storm drain and for a short distance Avondale Road acted as the western boundary.

The new plans effected another major adjustment. The new arrangement placed the original border planting outside the permanent grant, and consequently, hundreds of plants had to be transplanted to form another border line. This was not wholly accomplished until 1931. Excluded from the grant also were all the citrus groves except about twelve acres of Valencias planted in 1916, plus about eight acres of seedling oranges originally planted about 1875. The large concrete reservoir located at the foot of Hill Avenue was likewise outside the limits, as well as the new well adjacent to it, and another at the foot of Landor Lane. The latter was soon replaced with a twenty-inch well drilled near the intersection of Orlando and Oxford Roads and connected with the reservoir by a ten-inch pipe line over eleven hundred feet long.

One of the first improvements to the two-hundred-acre property was the 3,000-foot chain-link fence erected along the west boundary line. Approximately 12,000 lineal feet of a combination wall and fence, installed by our own crew of men, provided the remainder of the boundary evidence. Following the completion of these fences, 4,000 shrubs from our own nursery were planted between fence and curb, along the estate boundaries. A temporary fence along the southern border line and along the east line from the intersection of Stratford and Oxford Roads to the southeast corner was erected in 1929. It was replaced by a permanent wall and fence completed in July 1930, after which completion the entrance gate formerly placed on Huntington Drive was reset on Euston Road. Continuation of a matching fence and wall along Orlando and Oxford Roads to Stratford was not completed until 1932.

The Citrus Nursery

Soon after I was given the management of the citrus and other ranch properties, Mr. Huntington inquired as to the number of acres available for the extension of his citrus orchards. I recommended a maximum of 100 acres and suggested that we raise the trees in our nursery. In 1912 I planted the first seed to grow 20,000 trees, out of which we selected 10,000 of the strongest to be budded.

In 1916 we planted 85 acres in the following manner: the first ten acres received the choicest of the plants; the second ten was planted to the next best and so on, until the eighty-five acres had been completely planted, the last five acres receiving the smallest of the trees. After five years of observation, it was noted that the first and the second ten acres outgrew all the others, and came into the bearing stage sooner than the rest. Proportionate differences continued during the next five-year period of observation. I've always felt that it would have been of more than mere passing interest to have been able to observe the next ten years of growth also. But unfortunately the orchards were subdivided into residential lots shortly after the first ten years: this was on the property facing Orlando Road.

During Mr. Huntington's lifetime he was anxious to expand his citrus groves on the ranch to the extent of increasing his actual revenue-producing acreage. When the ranch began to pay for itself with its various products, he became very proud of the fact and took no little delight in telling his friends that he possessed an estate that actually paid for itself! Of course this was definitely an achievement.

Mother Nature, however, was to be reckoned with as far as financial success in this respect was concerned. The citrus fruits were occasionally exposed to unpredictable severe frosts, and consequently, the annual production could not be wholly depended upon. We were obliged to discuss the possibility of installing heaters for protection, but soon realized that there were many reasons why such a plan would not be feasible.

In the first place, we were located in the very center of a newly founded city when we began to consider this plan—a city with fine residential potentialities. The process of smudging our groves might discourage the establishing of the high-type residences we hoped to encourage. Secondly, the effect of the smoke and smudge from the heaters would very likely prove of considerable harm to the valuable paintings, tapestries, and other art objects already placed in the Huntington home, to say nothing of the effects upon the rare books and manuscripts to be housed in the contemplated new library building. The scheme, therefore, was abandoned in favor of a less attractive one, possibly, but a more practical one—that of readjusting property lines and disposing of the acreage through the Huntington Land and Improvement Company.

Miscellaneous Plant Collections

A collection of Oriental persimmons was started when the United States Department of Agriculture offered us some. This aroused the interest which led to the planting of ten acres of Hachiya and two acres of Fuyu persimmons. From government sources also we secured a collection of wine and table grapes which proved most satisfactory, as well as a collection of Chinese jujubes which are still in existence, and various nut trees, such as pistachio and pecans. A variety of fruits from Mexico and Central and South America was also tried; they included sapotas, bananas, mangos, and papayas (the latter proved too tender). Chestnuts, too, were planted, and from North Africa we obtained bud wood of the improved types of carob trees. About this time also the South American pineapple guava made its way to Southern California, and we gave two acres to it as a trial.

Experiments conducted with ornamental plants of many kinds were too numerous to describe. Among the grand total of some 50,000 plants embracing nearly 7,000 species and varieties which our files now record, many were planted over the years for the purpose of testing their suitability to our Southern California weather. Some proved adaptable; others failed the severer tests; and still others were discarded entirely. Experiments are still under way at this time of writing, 1948-49, and a few new ones have been instituted in the recent years—for example, the camellia test-garden. The latter should prove beneficial to many growers besides ourselves, especially in helping to clarify the nomenclature in this particular field.

[101]

A Reservoir

The requirements of the extensive ornamental plantings in addition to the many young citrus orchards necessitated an expansion of the water system by 1916. A new reservoir site, therefore, was soon determined upon: at the foot of Hill Avenue, which was the highest spot available at the time. We drilled a new twenty-inch well about the same time. The reservoir was of re-enforced concrete, 185 feet in diameter, with a capacity of 2,500,000 gallons. A well at the foot of Landor Lane supplied water through an eight-inch pipe. A ten-inch cast-iron pipe distribution line was then installed to connect the irrigation systems. Some years later, when it was necessary to establish new boundary lines, the reservoir and the wells were found to be located outside the permanent boundaries.

Since the excluded portion of the ranch was subdivided into residential lots, the well at the foot of Landor Lane was abandoned and a new one drilled within the permanent acreage, near the intersection of Orlando and Oxford Roads. The new well had a twenty-inch casing diameter and was sunk to a depth of 505 feet. It produced approximately 1,000 gallons of water per minute. In addition to the reserve well in the canyon, this last well constructed should provide amply for any future irrigation needs of the two hundred acres set aside by the deed of trust executed by Mr. Huntington, and now known as the Huntington Library and Art Gallery and Botanical Gardens.

The Mausoleum

One day in 1919 Mr. Huntington confidentially advised me that he was planning to erect a mausoleum on the San Marino Ranch, as a final resting place for both Mrs. Huntington and himself. The present site was finally selected after extended consideration by Mr. Huntington of various other possible locations about the ranch: it is almost due north of the residence.

When the decision had been made, it was decided that the only immediate improvement to be undertaken was the grading of the property so that a circular road eventually could be laid around the site itself, which in turn was to be elevated by the surplus soil from the construction of the road. On completion of the latter, Mr. Huntington himself directed the planting of two white-barked, lemon-scented eucalyptus trees, and two of the evergreen weeping variety of Chinese elm. Three lovely oaks already growing there were left as part of the landscaping.

In 1925, about a year after Mrs. Huntington's death, Mr. Huntington commissioned John Russell Pope of New York City to design a suitable mausoleum that would be both earthquakeproof and a thing of beauty. During the autumn of 1926 we excavated for the laying of the foundation for this structure. William C. Crowell, contractor, then erected the re-enforced concrete structure which was the skeleton of the contemplated building. It was allowed to remain in this stage for six months to insure its being thoroughly cured before adding the marble.

Mr. Huntington was never privileged to see the completion of the mausoleum, for he died in May of 1927. Temporary interment was made in a cement vault in the same manner in which Mrs. Huntington's remains had been cared for, pending the building of the mausoleum. We had removed the cement vault containing Mrs. Huntington's remains before excavating for the permanent structure's foundation, and had interred it near the proposed site.

In May 1929, when the mausoleum was finally completed, the two bronze caskets were removed from the cement vaults, and in the presence of the immediate family they were interred in the permanent crypt during a simple burial ceremony.

The Brunner Tile and Marble Company was entrusted with the installation of the Colorado Yule marble as well as with the mosaic work to be done on the underside of the dome. In order to make further provision for safeguarding the structure against destruction by earthquake, it was suggested that each marble column be bored through the center to its entire length. In this opening was inserted a 1¼-inch brace rod which projected one foot into the structure at each end.

The carving of the bas-reliefs on the outer circle—symbolic of the four seasons of man's life, spring, summer, autumn, and winter—and of the angels on the sarcophagus, was commissioned to a well-known sculptor, John Gregory, who himself executed the models. He sent from New York three craftsmen, an Irish, a French, and an American carver, who carved the relief work after the marble slabs had been set in place. Mr. Gregory made a special trip from New York at the completion of the work to inspect it personally.

Eastman cipolin marble was used for the mosaic ceiling and the underside of the dome. Colorado Yule marble served for the sarcophagus, and cipolin for the carved marble band. The floor of the mausoleum is designed of Colorado Yule and cipolin combined.

Widening of the Drives

When Mr. Shorb designed the original drives through the estate, they were primarily to be used for the family carriages, so they were only about fifteen feet wide. Soon after my arrival at the San Marino Ranch, Mr. Huntington advised me that he was not desirous of widening the drives to any appreciable extent because they were to serve strictly for private use. Consequently, when need for further driveways arose I laid out additional sections to widths not exceeding seventeen feet, at the same time installing curbs and gutters along the sloping portions to take care of the winter storm waters.

In 1925, however, it was found desirable to have our crew of men undertake the task of widening the drives wherever at all possible to a width of twenty feet, and to install the required curbs and gutters. This project took several years to complete.

The first section to be widened under the new plan was the road leading north toward the Orlando Road entrance to the mausoleum. The following season the road to the mausoleum between the Orlando entrance and the residence was finished, complete with cement curbs and oil surfacing. In 1927 the improvement of the circle drive was begun in the section west of the Japanese garden. This operation was interrupted by the death of Mr. Huntington in May of that year, at which time the Library Trustees ordered all construction terminated immediately.

The main entrance drive was planted in 1914 with Mr. Huntington's favorite *Cocos plumosa* palms—purchased from Dietrich's Nursery in Montebello. The *Cocos plumosa* drive dividing the palm and cactus gardens was planted with trees procured some years earlier while I was on a trip to San Diego with Mr. Huntington. We had agreed to specimen planting along the various drives through the estate with a view not only to the picturesque effect but also to the testing of different types of trees for fitness in parkway and street landscaping. The following plantings were made: Himalayan Cedar Drive, to trees planted from seed raised on the ranch; East Drive, to Canary Island date palms; South Drive, to mixed planting including the curious Guadalupe Cypress with a double trunk; another to Guadalupe Island palms purchased from Edward Rust's Nursery in South Pasadena; and two others, one to Chinese Windmill palms with a low supplementary planting of North African heather and one to Cedars of Lebanon (*Cedrus Libani*).

Visitors

During the time the Huntingtons lived in their mansion many people of great prominence visited them. In 1917 Prince Paul Troubetskoy was a guest and during his visit he modeled a bust of Mr. Huntington. The actual clay modeling took place inside the house; but the plaster-of-Paris work was done on the loggia, where an aspect of utter disorder reigned during this latter process.

Princess Hatzfeldt, adopted daughter of the Collis P. Huntingtons, visited the Huntington family here for several weeks one season, bringing with her a personal maid. During her stay more than the usual number of social activities took place. Sir Joseph Duveen, with his valet, visited the family whenever he came to Southern California in connection with the sale of paintings or other art objects. Dr. A. S. W. Rosenbach of Philadelphia was also a guest at the home whenever a transaction regarding rare books or manuscripts was in the offing. Homer L. Ferguson, president of the Newport News Shipbuilding and Dry Dock Company, a Huntington concern, stayed at the home on several occasions. Early in 1924 Oswald Birley, a prominent English portrait painter, painted the portraits of Mr. and Mrs. Huntington which are now on display in the library building. Mr. Birley painted Mr. Huntington's portrait when the latter was under the doctor's care, at a time when a period of extended poor health was reflected in his features.

In 1916 we were requested to build a guest house of considerable size because Mrs. Huntington anticipated a visit from her son and his wife, of New York. Due to unavoidable events they were unable to come; twice she was disappointed in this manner. As a result the new guest house remained vacant for several years. However, it was finally revamped and later relocated to serve as a home for the Director of Research, Dr. Max Farrand, and Mrs. Farrand; it was ready for their occupancy the autumn of 1930.

Library Building

As early as 1918 Mr. Huntington began to consider a suitable location for the erection of a building to house his steadily growing library. There were already stored in a section of the fireproof garage five hundred boxes of books. In January of 1918 preliminary plans and an outline of the construction picture were submitted to him. But it was not until early in 1919 that architects Myron Hunt and H. C. Chambers completed the plans, and in July 1919 the contract for the structure was given to William C. Crowell of Pasadena.

The location which Mr. Huntington selected for the building was densely planted to shrubs and trees, particularly the southernmost portion. This close planting had been originally intended to screen the path leading to the office building. Now trees and shrubs had to be transplanted, with the exception of two very old and partially decayed oak trees which were removed.

With the aid of power equipment and trucks we excavated for the basement, removing approximately 5,000 cubic yards of the soil. The procedure at this time was very different from the time when we were obliged to use antiquated plows and scrapers while excavating for the Huntington residence in 1908. To expedite the delivery of the necessary building materials, the spur track was once more extended along the entire front of the building site. The structure itself was built entirely of re-enforced concrete and brick. It was completed the following year—1920; and was thenceforth known as the library. Its location satisfied Mr. Huntington's wish that it be conveniently near the house, but at sufficient distance to insure the privacy of the family residence.

The large room in this main building measured 33 by 110 feet, with a ceiling height of 35 feet. It was designed with a small balcony in the center panel of the west wall and was designated as a reading room. It was to be illuminated by three chandeliers. The present inappropriate lighting fixtures resulted from high pressure salesmanship, a method that rarely was effective in dealing with Mr. Huntington. The only entrance to the stacks was from this reading room through a heavy vault door, in front of which was installed a desk-counter for the convenience of delivering books as well as for control.

On March 18, 1927, this room was opened to visitors for the display of rare books and manuscripts. Once a year the room is used as an assembly hall in the observance of Founder's Day, a use only partially successful, however, due to the shape of the room and its poor acoustics.

One of the problems faced in finishing the interior of this library building was the scarcity of steel, or its prohibitive cost, at the close of World War I. For this reason, our own crew of men installed temporary wooden shelves in the catalogue room and in the basement. It was not until June 3, 1921, that the Art Metal Construction Company, of Jamestown, New York, was given the contract to construct steel stacks to be installed in a special wing of the library. These stacks were to be of the most modern construction, protected by hinged doors, each of which was to be designed with two panels of plate glass; and the aisles were to be floored with white carrara glass three quarters of an inch thick.

In March 1920 the first electric alarm system was installed, in the rare-book stack, by T. E. Milster of Los Angeles. The same year marked also the construction of the stone mantel in the Founder's Room, by George W. Reynolds of Los Angeles, and the letting of the contract for the installation of the heating system, to the E. O. Nay Company of Pasadena—three important milestones in construction contracting.

The Library Staff

Spring of 1920 found the progress of construction accelerated to such an extent that Mr. Huntington began to consider arrangements to provide for a trained library staff which could take up its duties as soon as the new structure would be advanced enough to receive books. He soon set into motion plans for transferring to California most of the library staff then working in his New York City home. Various factors, however, had to be considered: first, the transportation of the families and their household goods; second, the acute local housing shortage after World War I which prevented finding sufficient accommodations within reasonable distance of the library grounds. Such difficulties would be minimized if part of the staff could be selected from residents of Southern California. I searched the neighborhood for weeks in the hopes of locating accommodations to be vacant by the coming September or October, but with limited success. However, a few homes were made available through the aid of acquaintances, friends, or relatives and these took care of the situation temporarily. As a result, the library staff which had been working in the Huntington home at 57th Street and 5th Avenue, New York, moved to California soon after the completion of the library building.

Three house purchases were made to accommodate the newcomers. They were on the street then known as Lopez Street, now named Monterey Road, and were what were called "ready-cut" houses, anticipating the modern "prefabricated" type. All were located conveniently near the Oak Knoll car line. One small bungalow on Oak Knoll Avenue was also pressed into service, and the former Mayberry home was made available. The latter had been moved ten years previously from the top of the knoll, above the Old Mill, to a lot at the intersection of Oak Knoll Avenue and Lopez Street. Leslie E. Bliss, who at the time was Curator and later became Librarian, the position he holds today, occupied the Mayberry house for a period during those early years. It previously had served the purpose of housing the first school class of the San Marino school district and was San Marino's first City Hall.

In June 1920 the John Polachek Bronze and Iron Company of Long Island City contracted with Mr. Huntington for the two pairs of bronze doors to be used at the principal entrance to the library. In two respects these doors were disappointing. Mr. Huntington was dismayed to find that all the doors had been cast from one model whereas one of each pair should have been reversed to make them balance correctly. Furthermore they were made to be unlocked only from the inside. Mr. Huntington desired to have a lock on the outside as well, in order to save the steps required to go into the building by another entrance when the main entrance was locked. This outside lock, however, was not feasible due to the apparent fact that the portion of the panel designed to take a lock was on the wrong side of the door. If the doors had been cast from two models instead of one, this difficulty could have been avoided. As it was, insertion of a lock for outside use would only accentuate the error in the casting process. The idea, therefore, was finally abandoned.

Considerable delay attended the hanging of these bronze doors, largely due to a strike at the factory. Altogether, the work on the library building was an extended and costly matter, for in addition to the total cost for contracted work, Mr. Huntington expended about $40,000 for extra labor and material, under my direction.

The following year of 1923, a radical alteration was made which changed the aspect of the southern wall of this new building: the windows were filled in with brick and plaster, an action deemed necessary to eliminate the possibility of the natural light striking the books and manuscripts opened for exhibit. Of equal importance in taking this step was the fact that all of the new and existing plaster panels in that room were to be covered by a sound-absorbing material in order to improve the acoustics. Reverberation percentage there was found to be 6.8, which is a figure greatly in excess of accepted acoustical standards.

Following closely on the need for the first addition made to the library in 1927, which extended through the court between the east wing (*i.e.,* the catalogue room) and the center wing housing the rare-book stack, was a second addition made through the remaining court between the stack room and the west wing. The latter was used for the offices of the manuscript department and as a stack for manuscripts. Along the north side, another reading room was created, with stacks beneath and additional offices. The contract for this addition was let to W. C. Crowell, signed August 30, 1929. In detail it included the following: a reference reading room, 107'8"x37'10"x28' high; two offices each on the first and second floors, and rest rooms; a room for book stacks extending through the entire basement and measuring 139'2"x36'x13'4" high; a manuscript wing with two rooms for stacks, each measuring 110′x22′x8′; and a top floor for offices.

Installation of the ventilating and air-conditioning systems presented problems of confusion for the library staff and readers. It was necessary to cut thirty-seven openings through foundation walls which were twenty to thirty inches thick. The openings ranged from thirty to forty inches square. Provision had to be made also for four openings of door size, and twenty-six additional openings through partition walls. All of this work involved the use of pneumatic drills which, of course, caused such noise and dust as to be of considerable discomfort to both staff and readers. The work was protracted beyond ordinary expectations because of the exacting nature of the work involved, including the installation of precautionary alarm devices, a temporary but necessary measure.

The New Entrance and Gates

The original entrance to the ranch was located along the eastern boundary, north of the present intersection of San Marino Avenue and Euston Road. From there the estate road led in a westerly direction for about a quarter of a mile, whence it turned north and wound up the hill and west again to the Shorb residence.

This same approach was maintained by Mr. Huntington until 1914 when a new and more direct road was planned through the citrus orchard from Huntington Drive. It was not an easy task to wind a road through straight lines of citrus trees without seriously interfering with the irrigation system. We managed a compromise by constructing a drive in two straight sections and two curves.

This new road was twenty-five feet wide between curbs. Added to that were strips of lawn ten feet wide on each side. In the centers of these parallel strips of lawn were planted 156 *Cocos plumosa*. To complete this landscaping a hedge of *Viburnum suspensum* was planted, using 1,600 plants.

Mr. Huntington had acquired three sets of handsome wrought-iron gates from Beddington Park, Surrey, England. They had been in use since 1714 and were originally installed by Sir Nicholas Carew. One set of the three, we placed at the terminal of the road at Huntington Drive. A single gate was placed on Huntington Drive at the entrance to the superintendent's house, and another was used at the Pasadena entrance to the ranch at the intersection of Rosalind Road and Canyon Drive. A third pair was reserved for the north entrance on Orlando Road, and a fourth, which was a copy, was

[109]

installed at the service entrance off of San Marino Avenue. The third pair of originals was installed at a later date than the others, when Orlando Road was established.

Three gate lodges, consisting of stucco buildings with tile roofs, were built at Huntington Drive, Rosalind, and Orlando Roads when need for them arose. And later a small cottage was placed near the service entrance from San Marino Avenue. About the time Oxford Road was opened, a new entrance and road to the library building replaced the former spur track: at this entrance, too, a double set of gates was installed. Later Mr. Huntington bought a very beautiful wrought-iron gate, possibly of Italian design—the last of his purchases of entrance gates. This last was placed at the entrance of the drive leading to the mausoleum from the north.

During subsequent years the various gates suffered considerable damage on one occasion after another, especially after the estate was opened as a public institution. The damage was largely by auto vehicles, chiefly because of careless drivers during the night. The gate on Euston Road was severely damaged in this manner in 1932, and similar accidents occurred which left their marks on the gates at Orlando and Oxford Roads. The main entrance gate was once hit with such force by an automobile as to push the entire center panel inward three feet. The side entrance gates at the same location have had to be repeatedly repaired due to damage done by sightseeing busses.

When the new boundary lines were established the main entrance gate to the ranch was moved from Huntington Drive to Euston Road, where it is today. The gate at Rosalind Road was sold with a section of land as an entrance to a new home-site. It was later purchased by Mrs. Edmund Burke Holladay, sister of Mr. Huntington, to be used as an entrance, appropriately, to the Collis P. and Howard Huntington Memorial Hospital. A duplicate was placed at Orlando Road to serve as an outlet to Pasadena. Along the eastern side, the service gate was finally abandoned as a new and wide gate, without an overhead section, served the purpose more satisfactorily. However, the former service gate is now part of the double gate located at the library entrance on Oxford Road.

The "Blue Boy"

Mr. Huntington's acquisition of Gainsborough's "Blue Boy" in 1921 was heralded country-wide by all newspapers. It was futile to attempt to keep the time of its arrival in San Marino a secret: reporters telephoned for information almost daily.

Generally paintings received through Sir Joseph Duveen were sent to San Marino by express. However, the importance of this particular portrait warranted that it be transported as personal baggage in the drawing-room of a Pullman car. I met the train on which Sir Joseph and his party were to arrive, and in the presence of many reporters and photographers, assisted in loading the box containing the canvas of the "Blue Boy" onto our truck.

To us this was just another occasion of one of Sir Joseph's visits during which it was customary for him to display for purchase a collection of paintings and art objects which he had collected from many corners of the world. His visits always involved considerable extra work of a very difficult and exacting nature, for it meant almost daily shifting of heavy, full-size paintings to different locations in the various rooms, halls and stairways of the Huntington home, so that the best effect would be secured. Sometimes Sir Joseph and Mr. Huntington exchanged art pieces so as to improve the latter's collection. More often new pieces were acquired whenever suitable room was available. Sir Joseph possessed an almost incredible ability in locating the exact and advantageous spot for the hanging of a new painting.

Such transactions as this would often consume about a week's time and they generally proceeded in the following manner: early in the forenoon the paintings were hung in the suggested places and for the balance of the day the family had the opportunity of viewing them thus. New arrangements or additions would be suggested and discussed. Weather permitting, the family and Sir Joseph would go for a drive into the country in the afternoon, sometimes joined by friends. Then over a cup of tea discussions would continue about the paintings. After dinner the conversation would invariably turn to the same topic, and suggestions would continue to be made, especially as to where and how the paintings were to be re-hung the next morning. Often these suggestions involved the re-hanging of certain items anywhere from three to twelve times, and following each change another round of inspection took place.

Almost without exception this was the procedure followed for days, or until a satisfactory decision had been made. At the conclusion of his visit Sir Joseph would board the train for New York, sometimes minus all of the art pieces he had brought for Mr. Huntington's careful consideration; occasionally he would return with certain pieces that he had accepted in exchange.

I remember only one shipment of art treasures other than the "Blue Boy" which had the distinction of being transported in the drawing-room of a Pullman car. Two of the most delicate and fragile statuettes made of terra cotta by the famous French sculptor, Clodion, were packed for shipment in two large suitcases, one to each case. The two men assigned to the trip were given strict orders not to allow anyone to carry the cases but themselves. They were further advised to take the cases to their drawing-room and to guard them in such manner that both men would not be absent from the room simultaneously. Fortunately for all concerned, instructions were followed to the letter, and upon arriving in Los Angeles, the men were met at the train and driven to the Huntington residence by car to insure the safe delivery of their precious cargo .

Mrs. Huntington's Death

On September 16, 1924, Mrs. Huntington died in New York after an illness lasting several months. Her remains were returned to California in the family's private car, "San Marino," accompanied by Mr. Huntington, his private secretary, and his house personnel. Her bronze casket was encased in a pine box; this proved to be too large to be carried through the car door when ready to be placed on the train. A large window had to be removed for its entrance, and the same procedure was followed when the casket was removed from the private car on its arrival in San Marino.

The remains were taken to a local mortuary to await final funeral arrangements. The service was held in the living-room of the Huntington residence, with Dr. Robert Freeman, minister of the Pasadena Presbyterian Church, conducting, and was attended only by members of the family and very intimate friends. The casket was then taken to the site selected for the mausoleum and was encased in a cement vault for temporary interment. Due to an all-night rain I had to change quickly arrangements made for the interment of the casket and for floral arrangements. Although the weather cleared in time for the service, a shelter had already been erected over the grave, a board walk laid to lead up from the road with overhead protection all the way, and the entire area decorated with plants, flowers, and greens.

First Christmas in San Marino

During Mrs. Huntington's lifetime the family always spent Christmas in New York, but in 1924, the first Christmas after her death, Mr. Huntington made plans for the first time to spend the holiday season in San Marino.

That particular Christmas Eve, the temperature was at freezing. Two crews of men had done everything possible to save a part of the orange crop, including use of newly installed orchard heaters. By ten o'clock Christmas morning, however, when I saw Mr.

Huntington to wish him a Merry Christmas, I was obliged to tell him—with considerable reluctance and no little embarrassment, that there was grave possibility of the loss of a $30,000 orange crop in areas not protected by the heaters. To all appearances he took the news in good spirit and then he walked over to the safe and from it took $450 in ten-dollar bills, handing them to me, to give each workman on the premises his share of this generous Christmas gift. Although I had been without sleep for the past twenty-four hours, due to the emergency, I made immediate contact with each man and extended Mr. Huntington's gift and good wishes for a Merry Christmas.

Mr. Huntington's Illness

Although Mr. Huntington's three daughters, who lived in the city of San Francisco, in Piedmont, and in Los Gatos, respectively, spent many weekends with him, he keenly missed the companionship of his late wife, Arabella. During the two years following her death, 1925 and 1926, he entertained many prominent visitors, a worthy and often expedient diversion in his loneliness. Among the well-known visitors who were entertained at San Marino Ranch were: John Drinkwater, English novelist and playwright; Otto H. Kahn, a New York banker of note; Mortimer Schiff, another New York banker; John D. Rockefeller, Jr., and his family; Sir Esme Howard, British Ambassador to the United States; Dr. A. S. W. Rosenbach of Philadelphia, an authority on rare books and manuscripts; Colonel Edward Everett Ayer, an internationally known collector and philanthropist; and the Crown Prince Adolf and the Crown Princess Louise of Sweden. For the latter guests, it had been the official welcoming committee's decision that the royal couple could not find a more delightful and appropriate place to remain during their visit in California. At the dinner given in their honor, many prominent persons from Los Angeles and Pasadena were present, including three of the Library Trustees and their wives. On that occasion Mr. Huntington escorted the Crown Princess to the dining-room, and Mrs. Holladay, Mr. Huntington's sister, who was acting as hostess, entered the dining-room on the arm of the Crown Prince.

It was during these years of Mr. Huntington's life that he acquired some of the most important portions of his collections, rare books, manuscripts, and paintings. The outstanding painting acquired was perhaps Sir Thomas Lawrence's portrait, "Pinkie." But Mr. Huntington was not at all in the best of health at this time: for some little while he had been under the care of his local physician, Dr. Ernest A. Bryant, who finally advised his patient to travel to Philadelphia to consult a specialist. When he was ready for the trip I noticed how depressed he was, and it was with an obviously heavy heart that he said to me in a voice filled with emotion, "Hertrich, if anything should go wrong, you know what to do." As we shook hands in farewell, his grip was firmer than ever before and he seemed reluctant to let go. I knew that he still had a number of things in mind which he had promised himself to accomplish during his lifetime, if possible.

Dr. Bryant, a nurse, and two servants left for Philadelphia in Mr. Huntington's private car, "San Marino." There he underwent an operation by Dr. John B. Deaver at the Lankeman Hospital. Upon returning to California he was more or less confined to his home under the constant care of physician and nurse, but still he managed to carry on personally a great part of his contemplated transactions.

NORTH ENTRANCE
TO MAUSOLEUM

*With detail of wrought-iron
gates, possibly Italian
in origin*

MAUSOLEUM *with trees chosen by Mr. Huntington*

MAIN ENTRANCE DRIVE *from Huntington Drive to the residence through the citrus grove*

SOUTH DRIVE, *leading from cactus garden to Japanese garden*

HIMALAYAN CEDAR DRIVE

DRIVE *planted to Guadalupe Island palms* (Erythea edulis)

COCOS PLUMOSA DRIVE, *between palm and cactus gardens*

NORTH DRIVE, *planted to rhododendrons, camellias, and tree ferns under native oaks*

COLLECTION OF CORDYLINES AND BEAUCARNEAS *about 1925*

The Memorial to Mrs. Huntington

In 1927 Mr. Huntington began to make arrangements with Sir Joseph Duveen to establish a memorial to Mrs. Huntington in the west wing of the library building, seemingly keenly aware at this time of the uncertainty of one's life span.

Sir Joseph arrived in California with two special express cars literally loaded with items: fine porcelain; statuettes of marble, bronze, terra cotta; and exquisite pieces of furniture and tapestries. We unloaded the cars at San Gabriel, unpacked the material, and set it in place for the preliminary inspection. There were a great many more pieces than were actually needed. For one entire week we placed, moved, replaced and removed most of the articles many times, until the final selection was made. After this, the balance of the material was repacked and reloaded in one car for the return trip to New York.

This mammoth transaction worked a noticeable strain on Mr. Huntington's somewhat precarious health. It would have worked a hardship on a healthy man to have consummated such a tremendous deal in so short a time. Aside from the more usual aspects of a business arrangement, this particular one involved the acceptance by Sir Joseph of a large tract of land as partial payment. The preliminary transaction regarding the land Mr. Huntington left up to me to negotiate: it was not until the second time Sir Joseph and I viewed the tract personally together that a satisfactory arrangement was agreed upon. This was the last, and definitely the largest transfer of art goods between Mr. Huntington and Sir Joseph Duveen.

Mr. Huntington's Death

As it gradually became apparent that Mr. Huntington was not making the desired recovery from his first operation, Dr. Bryant advised him to return to the Lankeman Hospital in Philadelphia for a thorough check-up by Dr. Deaver, who would be able to recommend any special care or attention that should be given.

Mr. Huntington's attitude was one of optimism and confidence in the successful outcome of his second trip to Philadelphia—a contrast to his feelings at the time of his first journey there in 1926; and he was obviously relieved that he had fully established a memorial to his wife, Arabella. As I bade him farewell on this second trip and wished him the best of luck and a safe return to the land he loved best, he replied with a broad and cheerful smile, "Thank you, Hertrich. I'll be as good as new when I return to San Marino; so in the meantime keep things moving—the same as always."

Once more, then, accompanied by Dr. Bryant, a nurse, and servants, the party left for Philadelphia on April 29, 1927. A second operation was performed by Dr. Deaver, but Mr. Huntington failed to rally and death followed shortly afterward. At his bedside were two of his daughters, Mrs. John B. Metcalf and Miss Marion Huntington; his sister, Mrs. Burke Holladay; and Dr. E. A. Bryant. His remains were returned to California in his private car, attached to a Union Pacific train at Chicago, transferred to the Southern Pacific at Colton, and then to the Pacific Electric at Shorb. The Pacific Electric engine was draped in black and bore a flag; it finally drew up to the spur track leading to San Marino Ranch, where the casket was transferred to a hearse in the presence of the family and of Troop No. 1 of the San Marino Boy Scouts standing at attention. This was on Saturday, May 28, 1927.

Funeral services were conducted by Dr. Robert Freeman in the large library room of the residence, at eleven in the morning on May 31st. Although the service was strictly private, the attendance of friends and business associates was more than the library could accommodate. Automobiles were parked on the lawn for lack of sufficient parking space. Hundreds of floral pieces from all over the country covered the library room and a tremendous overflow was taken directly to the grave. Pallbearers from among the ranch staff were selected on the basis of their long service with Mr. Huntington, and included: Gilbert Brown, John Gombotz, Paul Kley, Gabriel Florez, Sam Cockrell, Otto Veit, Jakob Müller, and George Chaplin. After the brief ceremony, members of the family and employees escorted the casket to its place of temporary interment next to Mrs. Huntington near the mausoleum which was under construction.

Living in the Huntington Residence

After the passing of Mr. Huntington, the family asked my wife and me to move into the residence until the return of the housekeeper, who was on a much-needed vacation. During this period, the state and federal authorities were busily engaged in taking an extremely detailed inventory for the purpose of computing the inheritance taxes.

Soon Mr. Huntington's heirs began a systematic division of the deceased's personal effects, with the exception of his priceless museum collection destined for public enjoyment. After the inheritance had been satisfactorily divided, the china, porcelain, crystal, silver, and linens had to be packed and labelled. Three of the largest vans obtainable from San Francisco were hired to transport some of the pieces to northern California where the three daughters lived. The contents of the wine cellar were handled exceedingly carefully: first I was obliged to secure a transfer license in accordance with the law, since this was the prohibition era. Then I purchased numerous five- and ten-gallon casks for the bulk wines stored in hogsheads. The five-gallon casks, after being filled, were packed into crockery barrels, and marked, CROCKERY—HANDLE WITH CARE. All of the bottled wines and liquors were packed in a similar manner. When the vans drew up to the residence to be loaded, I managed to have the movers first load on some furniture, to be followed by cases and crockery barrels, and lastly, more furniture. Thus the drivers were never aware, so far as we knew, of the more interesting contents of the load they were transporting, and the goods were delivered without mishap to their destinations, San Francisco, Piedmont, and Los Gatos.

Protection of Art Collections

While this period of readjustment was going on, steps were being taken by the Trustees of the Library to transform the Huntington residence into an art gallery so the public could be admitted according to previously conceived plans.

One of the first precautions to be taken was the installation of an electric burglar alarm system which would include every door, window, and ventilator from basement to roof. The installation of this system became a complicated affair due to the many openings—over 250—which had to be considered in the two main buildings. It took almost a year before the delicate contacts were so adjusted as to be dependable and in good working order. During that time many false alarms were sounded, due to one cause or another, such as expansion and contraction caused by changes of temperature, heavy winds, too fine adjustments, etc. My sleep was frequently interrupted since I insisted on being notified whenever an alarm occurred, false or otherwise: 146 such alarms sounded during that period of perfecting the installation, but it was an excellent opportunity for becoming acquainted with the entire mechanism. Special electric lines were ultimately laid directly to San Marino police headquarters and control stations, as part of the alarm system. The cable was installed in 1931.

The next important consideration was the safeguarding against theft, vandalism, and earthquakes. Of particular concern were all items of porcelain or china; clocks, statuettes, and vases; and other pieces either in the Huntington residence or in the Arabella Huntington Memorial room of the library. With the able and willing assistance of three members of my staff, we introduced many new and what proved to be practical ideas, assuring the protection of the more fragile items, especially against earthquake movements. The plain glass shelves in the exhibition cases were replaced with reinforced glass. All porcelain, china and crystal pieces were securely fastened to the shelves, by means of glue and a cushion of felt which was placed as a binder between the object and the shelf. Bronze, marble, and terra-cotta statuettes exhibited on pedestals or stands were made secure in many ingenious ways.

Some of the precautionary methods used were as follows: pedestals were securely anchored to the floor or wall and then fastened to a support in ways depending upon the delicacy of the item concerned. Glass exhibition cases of delicate construction, and fine furniture pieces, were fastened to floor or wall, depending again upon location. Items on marble shelves above the fireplaces were secured to the marble or wall board behind. Glass shelves supporting the valuable porcelain vases in the art gallery exhibition cases were further re-enforced with chromium steel straps and the brackets then strengthened with heavy piano wire.

After the Compton-Long Beach earthquake in 1933, additional methods were devised for protection of the valued art pieces. One was the installation of steel plates in the back of all paintings and tapestries. In rooms having wood paneling, the plates were fastened to the panels. Considerable difficulty was encountered where paintings and tapestries were supported by plaster on tile walls. Finally a system was devised to overcome this particular problem by fastening the heavy plate on half-inch steel straps which were four inches wide and suspended from concrete beams. This was achieved during 1934 and 1935.

Enlarging the Cactus Garden

During the time the citrus orchards to the south of the Huntington estate were being subdivided into residential lots, the large open reservoir at the foot of the cactus garden was abandoned. Surplus soil accumulating from the grading of the streets in this new subdivision was used to fill in the reservoir and the surrounding low section. This added to the Huntington grounds approximately four acres which could be planted further with cactus and other desert plants.

In order to create an immediate and effective display in this newly added area, we were obliged to transplant numerous large specimens of plants established earlier—some of them weighing between two and five tons. Included among these were South African aloes, Mexican yuccas, dasylirions, nolinas, some century plants (*i.e.,* agaves), and a few South American cereus.

Over the period of years since the establishment of this desert garden, we had accumulated what was considered the largest collection in the world of desert specimens planted out-of-doors. In order to maintain a live collection of such plants, it was necessary for us to make replacements from time to time—by propagation, exchange with other plant collectors, and by purchase—since each year material was lost by frost, disease, or old age. Mr. Huntington became very proud of the recognition of the worth of this garden to horticulturists, not only in the United States but also in South America, Europe, Africa, and Australia.

Fortunately for our collection, several other desert garden enthusiasts, including Arthur Letts, discontinued their private gardens for various reasons and so some of the choicest species from several of the gardens found a permanent home in the Huntington Botanical Gardens. In 1928, a trip to Europe resulted in my locating a number of rare plants to enrich our collection, and a second trip ten years later produced equally gratifying results. The latter resulted specifically in acquisition of rare South American and South African desert plants, plus promise of extended exchange of further material in the future, a promise faithfully borne out when circumstances have permitted. We ourselves had much plant material at that particular time to offer in exchange for what we were receiving from other botanical gardens.

Some years prior to Mr. Huntington's passing, Mrs. John D. Wright of Montecito began to collect cactus on a very large scale. She spared neither expense nor effort, and as a consequence, in a very short time she had assembled a most remarkable collection. In 1941 when the Wrights decided to move to New York, we acquired from them some of the more interesting specimens. And in 1942 Mrs. Wright donated to the Huntington Botanical Gardens about 100 of her rare plants.

Albert Mendel of Hollywood, another enthusiastic cactus grower, passed on in 1940, whereupon his son, W. Mendel, gave to our gardens the larger portion of his father's worthy collection. Such reminiscences of this type of plant collecting over the past years is most interesting now in the light of the fact that after competing with about a dozen other ardent collectors, in the end most of the rarer specimens found permanent places in the Huntington collection.

A major problem that presented itself in connection with the above activities in establishing this specialized type of garden collection was how to allow the general public into that section, which was laid out with small beds and narrow paths. This particular type of planting had been followed because in the beginning Mr. Huntington had long remained open to conviction as to the wisdom of such a garden at all. It was not until I had developed it bit by bit, and it had become well known the world over, that he began to feel considerable pride in having so unusual a set-up, which by that time was the envy of many a collector of cactus and succulent specimens.

Many of the paths of this section had been laid out so that a close inspection could be made of the plants as individuals, at the same time providing efficient drainage which is so essential to this type of plant. It was a difficult job to devise a plan whereby this large area divided into many small beds could be efficiently guarded against theft, injury or vandalism.

At the beginning visitors were allowed only to the lower boundaries, but the interest was so great that it was deemed advisable to extend the privilege to other sections. In 1930 materials were secured that made possible the laying of a walk 1,100 feet long and 10 feet wide to lead through the center of the garden, running north and south. During that summer five carloads of desert lava rock were obtained and a rockery was constructed. Into this substance was planted a representation of the general species and varieties. It was an arrangement that proved satisfactory to both the visitors and ourselves, for it represented a balanced planting of the specimens and also eliminated to a great degree the difficulty of guarding the entire cactus garden. To add further to the public's edification and pleasure 3,000 metal labels were placed on the outstanding plants here and elsewhere, providing botanical information.

Huntington Land and Improvement Company

Following the passing of Mr. Huntington, I continued to supervise ranch properties belonging to the Huntington Land and Improvement Company on a cost-plus basis, the Library deriving the benefit from this arrangement. During the first year this company was charged $26,649.57 for services rendered, and corresponding sums were charged as the acreage of the properties decreased in succeeding years.

Before San Marino Ranch was reduced to 207 acres in area, the returns from the sale of citrus fruits and other crops amounted to a considerable sum of money per year; but this was reduced to a fraction thereof after the new boundary line was established.

Returns from the citrus, avocado, and persimmon trees even then, however, were notable. The value of ornamental plants planted on residential lots for the Huntington Land and Improvement Company amounted to $11,655.34 during the season of 1928-29.

From Private Estate to Public Institution

The transformation of Mr. Huntington's estate to an institution that could be opened to the public involved a somewhat extended procedure. Responsibility for placing the buildings of the estate and its art treasures under institutional control, however, was accomplished under the chairmanship of Henry M. Robinson with commendable dispatch.

Mr. Robinson had been a frequent caller at the Huntington home during the latter years of Mr. Huntington's lifetime, and he had therefore become very well acquainted with the general plan that Mr. Huntington had in mind with regard to his beloved ranch. Following Mr. Huntington's passing, Mr. Robinson, vice-chairman of the board of trustees, took a very active interest in the responsibilities placed upon that board, George S. Patton, the chairman, being ill at the time. Mr. Robinson made frequent trips to the institution, spending considerable time there on Saturdays, and occasionally surveying activities on Sundays.

During the time the Huntington family occupied the residence, the gardens were not open to visitors, save on rare occasions. Mrs. Huntington's gravely impaired eyesight prevented her from enjoying the garden with guests in a normal fashion. When Mr. Huntington realized that the gardens were becoming a botanical and horticultural mecca for students in these fields, he sought guidance in supplying pertinent information regarding the plants under cultivation. The many exotic plants that had been assembled were of use and pleasure to the family, but they also were the beginning of a collection that would serve as a natural laboratory in which could be tested the adaptability of certain species to the Southern California climate. It became increasingly obvious that it was necessary to have all plants labelled. The multitude of exotic specimens, after all, would tax the knowledge of even a trained horticulturist, which Mr. Huntington did not claim to be, lover of plants though he was. Labels were made for his convenience and an additional 3,000 were prepared in 1929-30 for the public visitors to the gardens, giving common and scientific names, notation of the plant families to which each plant belongs, and finally, serial numbers for filing purposes.

Due to the shortness of time during which the change was to be made to open the buildings and grounds to the public, the conversion of facilities presented a difficult assignment, with the limited staff at hand. Consequently, at first only a small portion of the grounds was open, but in succeeding months, as quickly as additional areas were made ready and provision made for properly guarding them, they were thrown open, to include the cactus garden and the Japanese garden.

The year following the official opening of the grounds, a new approach to the mausoleum was landscaped, shortening the distance from the public entrance from 3,200 to 1,700 feet. The new walk, leading from the east, was ten feet wide, bordered on either side with a panel of lawn twenty-five feet wide. Records show that some two hundred visitors each day availed themselves of the opportunity to view the resting place of Mr. and Mrs. Huntington.

It was early realized that converting the estate into a public institution necessitated planning specific conveniences to add to the public's comfort. Parking areas were needed within the premises to eliminate the inconvenience of overcrowding the city streets just outside the entrance to the grounds. Public rest rooms were provided. Areas in the grounds and buildings not yet available for public viewing were roped off or otherwise protected. All of this work within the buildings required much care, and it took six months' time of four of the best men on my staff before we felt security in our system of protection.

Miscellaneous adjustments of a widely varied nature had to be considered. One was conformity with the state regulations pertaining to public buildings with regard to doors: all doors leading to the outside had to be rehung to open outward. It was deemed necessary to discontinue the water supply above the first floor to eliminate all possible source of damage to the art treasures on the lower floor. At the time the residence was built in 1909, there was insufficient water pressure for the fixtures on the second and third floors due to the low elevation of the then available reservoir. An overhead tank system in the attic supplied the need, but this was immediately discarded when the residence was converted into an art gallery. Another change that required considerable effort was the relocation of the bindery equipment set up at Mr. Huntington's request some years previous. The photostat and photography department was expanding so rapidly that there was not adequate room for both in the basement of the library building, where they were originally set up. Expansion of activities in the bindery department was also anticipated, so it was moved bodily to the garage. The north portion of that building was "temporarily allocated" for that purpose, but now after nineteen years the "temporary" arrangement is still in effect: the garage is still harboring the bindery activities.

Guards for Exhibits

All members of the household personnel and grounds staff were given the opportunity of accepting positions under the new set-up; the majority took advantage of this offer. It had been estimated that in order properly to guard the exhibitions twenty men and two women would be required to act as guards during the afternoons which were scheduled to be open to the public. Gradually this number had to be increased as the number of visitors increased until a maximum of thirty guards was reached—a number maintained until the necessity for economy in 1938 brought about a reduction in the ranks until there were only fourteen. It was because of this latter condition that a decision was made in April of 1940 to close the road to the mausoleum, since this would eliminate the need for two guards stationed there. This was regrettable because so much interest had been shown in the mausoleum: 46,205 people had been checked that first season the road was opened, on their way up the third-of-a-mile walk to the imposing structure. After the closing of the road an effort was made to keep accurate count during one month of the number of inquiries about its reopening: result, 2,465.

During the days of heaviest attendance of visitors, it is remembered that the institution at one time inaugurated a tallying system whereby the guards at the entrance doors to each building by means of two checkers, one for incoming and one for outgoing visitors, were able to regulate the flow to avoid overcrowding, a condition that might make the safeguarding of valuable objects an uncertainty. When the strict economy measures in later years were in order, one of the precautions taken was to encase each of the statuettes in the Arabella Huntington Memorial in transparent cylinders of lucite. Special efforts were made to feature certain garden attractions at this time to relieve traffic through the buildings if possible. Recording of this experiment showed that when the gardens offered particular attractions, a good many visitors went to the gardens only, which mitigated to some extent the hazard of overcrowding the gallery and library building.

When the system of guards was instituted, the matter of procuring suitable persons for this responsible work was a problem, chiefly due to the fact that guards were needed only part time, since the grounds and buildings were to be opened only during the afternoon. After giving the matter thoughtful consideration, I decided to select the guards from the grounds and buildings personnel—people whom I knew to be most reliable and trustworthy. Some of these men and women were former house servants who thoroughly appreciated the value and importance of guarding the items in their charge. By and large this proved a most successful procedure: represented among the personnel in the new set-up were comparatively young men and women who were efficient in every respect.

For the convenience of these members of the grounds staff pressed into this new type of service as guards following their regular hours of a different type of work in the morning, we built dressing rooms and showers. And in 1928 the servants' recreation cottage was enlarged to provide for Miss Nora N. Larsen and her sister Julia, both of whom had served many years in the Huntington household. They were about to assume their new responsibilities and required appropriate living quarters: Miss Nora Larsen took over the management of tea and lunch rooms, and her sister accepted the position of guard and caretaker in the art gallery.

In 1933 when the servants' wing was dismantled to make room for a new gallery, the showers and dressing rooms for the guards were moved to a new building erected near the business office. Some difficulty admittedly attended the employment of a full corps of young men who could qualify as efficient workers during the forenoons and as courteous, efficient guards in the afternoons, because the wage scale at that time (*i.e.,* shortly after the estate was opened to the public) provided only fifty cents an hour for these employees, with little prospect for advancement in either opportunity or salary.

An almost continuous program of change, alterations or additions was kept up during these early days of service to the public in order to meet the exigencies created by that public. Check rooms had to be established because regulations had been made by the trustees that would not permit cameras, umbrellas, canes or miscellaneous packages or articles to be carried into the exhibition rooms. For the convenience of enquiring patrons we established also a sales desk, where guidebooks, catalogues, and other literature were offered. Various locations were tried for these conveniences, though even at this time of writing no thoroughly satisfactory arrangement has been devised. Space was allocated in 1931, in an attempt to better the existing conditions, in the west room of the main building of the library, for both the sales desk and adjacent check room. The same year the check room in the art gallery was changed from near the north entrance to the small library room next to the loggia entrance from the east. A second change was made in 1938 when the combined sales activities were established in the passageway between the former dining room and the new gallery.

Soon after the opening of the Arabella Huntington Memorial it became obvious that additional ventilation was needed. A separate system to take care of this need was installed. The first attempt to install suction fans on the roof resulted in too noisy an apparatus, however, and a set of rotary ball-bearing ventilators was subsequently ordered and installed. The latter in turn had to be removed after the Pearl Harbor incident because all skylights had to be replaced with five-inch-thick concrete slabs.

Another operation occasioned by increase in attendance of visitors was that of providing parking space for their automobiles. Several times further areas were allotted, and space for staff and grounds personnel had to be increased, as the library staff grew from twenty-five to fifty-two members, and twenty more parking stalls became necessary to accommodate groundsmen and guards.

It is interesting to note at this point the many states of our Union represented among visitors to the exhibitions. To satisfy my curiosity I instructed the guards in charge of the parking of cars to make a careful day-to-day check-up during the summer of 1932. The results were as follows: from Alabama 2, Arizona 56, Arkansas 4, California 15,892, Colorado 81, Connecticut 18, Florida 6, Georgia 3, Idaho 15, Illinois 134, Indiana 35, Iowa 46, Kansas 37, Kentucky 6, Louisiana 3, Maine 12, Maryland 9, Massachusetts 38, Michigan 67, Minnesota 52, Missouri 35, Mississippi 8, Montana 24, Nevada 9, New Hampshire 10, New Jersey 23, New Mexico 13, New York 109, North Carolina 2, North Dakota 23, Ohio 85, Oklahoma 21, Oregon 85, Pennsylvania 30, Rhode Island 2, South Dakota 19, Tennessee 2, Texas 71, Utah 50, Vermont 6, Virginia 4, Washington 145, West Virginia 2, Wisconsin 34, Wyoming 13, District of Columbia 17; Canada 47, France 1, Hawaii 1, Canal Zone 1, Mexico 3. The grand total of domestic and foreign cars during that summer season was 17,441.

The Tea Room

Soon after the estate was opened to visitors, frequent requests came to us of a nature that made it seem desirable to provide facilities for refreshments and relaxation during the visiting hours, as well as for lunches for our own staff. In 1929 the building formerly housing the billiard room and bowling alley underwent alterations to provide the following accommodations: a tea room to be opened to visitors, two dining-rooms, one for staff use and the other designated as the directors' dining-room; a pass-pantry, a kitchen, and a store room.

The bowling alley was the portion converted into the staff and research workers' luncheon room, and the billiard room was furnished to serve as a lounge room where visitors to the exhibitions could rest and be served afternoon tea. Twenty-four round tables were provided, and seventy-five chairs, as equipment to care for the average of ninety-seven outside visitors who were found to patronize the tea room daily. For the greater convenience of the regular corps of staff members, another room was added later to the east side of this building, and later still another on the west side.

During the first few months that the tea room was opened to the public, we realized that the accommodations were going to be inadequate, as requests came for use of the rooms for private afternoon parties. To help meet this situation, a pair of French doors in the partition separating the public room from the adjacent directors' room was soon installed. Altogether there was great enthusiasm shown for these conveniences, and yet, in spite of the popularity of the tea room, the first three months of operating showed a loss of $5.00 per day, which decreased gradually to $1.30 per day at the end of the first year. As time went on, a combination of circumstances necessitated discontinuing tea room service for the public, the chief of which was securing efficient personnel for the few hours of afternoon work required. But before the tea room was closed the deficit had been made up.

Further Improvements

During the season of 1930-31, various improvements were made for further efficiency of operation both in the buildings and on the grounds. The superintendent's office was enlarged to provide additional space for the rapidly increasing horticultural library. In the main office a new and enlarged switchboard was installed for the extension of service that was found to be necessary.

In the engineering field, the following improvements were made: a sixteen-inch drain pipe was laid which led from the east side of the library building to Oxford Road; and under the road surface through the Oriental garden, a twenty-four inch storm drain was constructed. In the same area a circulating pump was installed to provide moving water over the falls in the Oriental garden.

The Horticultural Library

The horticultural library grew up from infant size in much the same gradual way as the collection of plants in the garden. When we first began to collect plants, Mr. Huntington promised to supply me with books on botanical subjects: horticulture, agriculture, forestry and allied subject matter. For the most part we accumulated such material a little at a time, though a few items were purchased *en bloc,* such as those from the Hoe and Poor libraries.

After World War I, I was able to add important works by direct purchase, namely: *Allgemeine Gartenzeitung, Botanische Zeitung,* and a complete set of *Curtis's Botanical Magazine,* all of which contain valuable original descriptions of plants. In a specialized field, the *Kakteenkunde* was a most welcome addition as a source of information on cactus and other succulent plants. The acquisition of a complete set of the *Gardeners' Chronicle* of England and the Kew *Bulletins* I considered most fortunate— two hundred and fifty volumes and more, all told. Mention should also be made of the valuable Missouri Botanic Gardens annual publications, the writings of Dr. Engelmann edited by Trelease, and of William Trelease himself; a set of Engler and Prantl, of *Addisonia,* of Paxton's *Botany* and Edwards and Lindley's *Botanical Register; Flora Australis;* the important works on the genus Eucalyptus by Baron von Mueller, and by Maiden; Barbosa Rodrigues' *Sertum Palmarum Brasiliensium* and *Flora Capensis.* Added to these are complete sets of the California Avocado Association's *Yearbook,* of *Citrograph,* and the *Cactus and Succulent Journal of America,* periodicals of sound reference value; as well as various noteworthy works on orchids, including a de luxe copy of *Reichenbachia.*

These sets are, of course, only a portion of the library collection: to name all would require a special file, but mention should be made of some of the outstanding gifts of the Friends of the Huntington Library to this department. Such include the early Fuchs's *Herbal;* the *Silva of North America* by Sargent; Ravenscroft's *Pinetum Britannicum;* and H. Clinton-Baker's *Illustrations of Conifers.*

Many books in the library I received from Mr. Huntington and other individuals who appreciated my efforts to assemble a worthy library. One in particular who knew of my wish to augment our collection of palms was Captain H. A. Johnston of London, an ardent student of these particular plants: he sent me a set each of *Webbia* and *Malesia.*

This horticultural library has been of inestimable assistance in studying the plant material of our gardens, and it will continue to be so in the future, not only to our own personnel but to visiting students of botany and horticulture, and to a great many earnest amateur plant lovers. It has always been housed in the office of the superintendent to make it available for quick reference. If this specialized library were housed in the general reference stacks it would be out of reach at times when it would be most needed. Live specimens of plants are frequently brought in from the gardens for study —a practice that would be most distracting for readers in the general reference reading rooms. Research work in connection with live plant material, of a nature such as we are confronted with, for instance, in identification processes, must necessarily be considered as a working unit separate from the type of work carried on in the main library and art gallery buildings.

The slow but steady increase in volumes in the botanical collection of books made it advisable in 1930 to provide more room for them. Two rooms were added to the office building at that time, which gave the superintendent and his staff much needed additional room for carrying on their work. Unfortunately, the addition was of a temporary nature insofar as it was not fireproof, because it was anticipated that a permanent structure was to be built at a later date. The "temporary" quarters, however, are still in use.

The Plant Catalogue

Since 1928, when the Botanical Gardens were first opened to the public, requests have continued to come in through the superintendent's office for information pertaining to the collection of plants under cultivation. The *Guide to the Desert Plant Collection,* published in 1939, was very well received, but requests for information about other plants, particularly the lesser known exotics, still were unanswered. Labels had been placed wherever practical, carrying identification data, but it was cultural data and other details that could not be covered in labels that visitors sought. Such material could be briefly stated in a catalogue, preferably of pocket size.

In 1938 I started preparation for such a catalogue by installing a card index of all material on hand. Next I began to prepare a file of hundreds of photographs to illustrate the more interesting specimens, and the lesser-known species, in flower if possible. Over a period of fifteen years I photographed thousands of plants and flowers in black and white for reproduction, also some in natural color. These have been available for use in educational work in the community. To photograph palms, cycads, trees and shrubs presented no special problems because their flowering periods last for days, weeks, or months. However, when it came to photographing the night-blooming cereus, the operation had to take place between 5 and 6 A.M.; and with other specimens similar problems presented themselves.

The preparation of a catalogue of this type, embracing all or most of the plants in the extensive botanical collection, involved considerably more time than I could devote to such a project, in connection with the many other responsibilities of superintendency. Consequently, to date only the preliminary data are prepared. Since my retirement in 1947, however, more time is becoming available and preparations are going ahead to supply public demand with respect to this catalogue material.

Annoyances

It was during the summer of 1937 that we located a heavy infestation of termites in the art gallery building. They were found to be coming from beneath the floor of the large drawing-room. Since a large portion of the sub-floor and supports had been completely destroyed, we were obliged to take the stringent measure of removing the large French window and frame, and a section of the parquetry floor as well. When about fifty square feet of tile wall had been taken away we discovered a huge asbestos nest, containing thousands of these destructive pests, located between the inner and the outer walls. Originally the asbestos had been used as a sound-absorbent medium for concealed water spouts, but apparently there had been a long-standing leak through a break in the copper pipe which caused the asbestos to disintegrate. As a result, the accumulation of this moist material on the first floor level had been providing an ideal home for these insects.

A similar condition was evident in one of the basements of the library building, and we discovered it at about this same time. Termites were emerging from beneath the concrete flooring along supporting columns. To eliminate them, we drilled 450 holes in the floor slab at the point of their emergence and forced gas under pressure into each opening to a depth of three feet. This method of expelling the pests proved so successful that we have not had a recurrence of the trouble.

One of the most aggravating of situations occurred when the main sanitary sewers to the art gallery clogged in 1941. Several hundred feet of this particular sewer had been installed beneath the heavy concrete basement floor, entering the building under the foundation walls about fourteen feet below the terrace floor.

We were obliged to break through the concrete at several places before the difficulty was located. Below the south terrace we found that the roots of a bignonia vine had grown through a section of broken clay pipe and its roots had completely filled two entire lengths of the pipe. Using the less expensive clay pipe in place of the more substantial cast-iron pipe proved to be a costly error in construction. It took five men one whole week to repair the line, recast the concrete slabs, dig a tunnel under the terrace, and replace the clay pipe with cast iron.

LIBRARY BUILDING *under construction, 1919*

LIBRARY BUILDING AND PLANTING *as it appeared immediately after completion*

THE ARCHITECTS' DRAWING
for the present main exhibition room

MAIN EXHIBITION ROOM OF LIBRARY BUILDING *after it was opened to the public*

LIBRARY BUILDING *before the south windows were closed in*

LIBRARY BUILDING *after the south windows were closed in*

MR. HUNTINGTON BEFORE THE BRONZE DOORS OF THE LIBRARY

MAIN ENTRANCE GATES AT SAN MARINO RANCH *on Huntington Drive, about 1917*

ORIGINAL SETTING OF THE GATES

*Beddington Park, Surrey, England, where they were installed by
Sir Nicholas Carew in 1714*

[143]

TABLE SET FOR A DINNER

*Given for the Crown Prince and Prin-
cess of Sweden, July 23, 1926.
Copyright by Boyé*

STAIRCASE OF THE RESIDENCE

Shortly after it was opened to the public

MR. HUNTINGTON *on the steps of the porte-cochere*

NEW WING OF ART GALLERY

Where some of the most famous paintings now hang

ADDITION TO THE CACTUS GARDEN

This represents the location of the former reservoir, discontinued and filled in about 1925

GIANT CACTUS *transplanted from the Arizona desert when the cactus garden was enlarged (the glass house was constructed around the base of the plant in order to encourage root growth during cold weather)*

CEREUS ALACRIPORTANUS, *weighing 6000 pounds, transplanted*

CEREUS XANTHOCARPUS, *from Paraguay, weighing about eight tons*

COCOS PLUMOSA DRIVE *overlooking the desert garden*

**FROST
DAMAGE
TO YOUNG
ORANGE TREES**
1922

*Some of them were saved
by binding the trunks
immediately following the
first frosty night*

One of the "unusual" aspects of California. Part of the gardens after the snow of January 11, 1949

WILLIAM HERTRICH—*at his desk in the horticultural library*

The New Gallery

The year of 1932 marked the culmination of conferences and reports regarding the urgent need to house some of the most valuable paintings and art objects in a special building to be constructed as nearly damageproof as humanly possible.

The Santa Barbara earthquake of 1925 had caused some startling discoveries to be made regarding the type of buildings known to be most resistant to earthquake shock. The Huntington home was closely scrutinized with this in mind: it had been built of re-enforced concrete frame, with filler walls of hollow tile, a construction that would doubtless be subject to damage in case of a severe earthquake.

When I conveyed this unnerving piece of information to Mr. Huntington, he took it under serious consideration and fully intended having the matter thoroughly investigated, but due to his failing health he neglected to follow through with this and he died before any substantial result came of my recommendation.

In 1928 I brought up the subject again, this time with Henry M. Robinson, Chairman of the Board of Trustees. After repeated warnings about the urgency of the matter, the Trustees decided to consult with the well-known geologist, Dr. J. P. Buwalda; the eminent geophysicist, Dr. Beno Gutenberg; and Professor R. R. Martel, structural engineer, all of the California Institute of Technology, as well as with Myron Hunt, the architect of the Huntington residence.

In May 1932 the combined reports of these experts motivated plans for the construction of a new wing in the art gallery. It took the place of the former servants' quarters, which were wrecked in September and October of that year—an operation that caused some concern because pneumatic drills and hammers had to be used, causing a fine dust to fly which would be injurious to the art objects inside, were it allowed to penetrate into the art gallery. The precautionary measures taken to avoid this hazard were a major operation in themselves. It involved sealing all windows, doors, ventilators, and air intakes, with the exception of one entrance, with glued paper. Added to this precaution was the installation of burglar alarms on all openings, new and old, between the west wing and the main building.

Before demolishing the servants' wing, experiments were conducted to test the strength of the type of construction of this art gallery building. They were carried out through the supervision of Professor Martel. Heavy timbers were set against the north side of the building at an angle of about forty-five degrees, and by means of hydraulic jacks pressures to approximately fifty tons were exerted. This caused some of the columns to crack and a few of the walls to collapse.

[155]

While the work was being done on the new wing, the former west wing was undergoing renovation and strengthening also, and provision was made on the first floor for exhibition space, while the second floor was arranged to accommodate other art collections and also the art library. Further precautionary measures against earthquake were taken at this time with regard to all chimneys above the roof line of the art gallery. This would be a protection for the buildings themselves and also for visitors: the heavy (one and a half to two ton) concrete chimney caps set on top of the hollow-tile supports were replaced by dummies made of sheet-iron, reducing the weight to about three hundred pounds each. In case of earthquake anyone walking beneath these chimneys would have been gravely endangered by the chimney caps falling to the balcony or the terrace below, as might conceivably happen with the crumbling of the supports.

A final step in these operations on the new wing was the wiring of the new gallery for the electric burglar alarm system and its equipping for air-conditioning. Following the completion of the entire project, Curator Maurice Block selected twenty-two paintings to be hung in the new 40 x 80-foot room under as ideal conditions as could be provided with regard to lighting, temperature, and humidity. The only fault found when the room was opened for exhibit was the noise of the air-conditioning machinery. This was soon rectified by cushioning the mechanical parts with timber and felt. The new gallery was formally opened to visitors on June 10, 1934.

It is a curious fact to note here that Mr. Huntington carried very little insurance on his properties. In reply to my inquiries he would say: "I have too many interests to insure them all; it is less expensive to carry my own." This I could understand, but could not visualize the risk he took in not properly safeguarding his priceless art treasures against possible damage by earthquake, in view of the fact that he knew of the considerable loss suffered in the Collis P. Huntington home in San Francisco from earthquake in 1906. Perhaps he considered his San Marino home to be sufficiently resistant to fire and earthquake. If he had conferred with Sir Joseph Duveen on the subject, I am reasonably certain that Sir Joseph would not have recommended any additional precautions to those normally taken, since his experience was naturally based on the consideration of museums in countries not subject to earthquakes.

That buildings of structure similar to the Huntington residence could suffer considerable damage from this type of natural catastrophe was borne out not only in the Santa Barbara earthquake in the 1920's but also in the more recent one suffered in Long Beach. This presented a very definite problem to the Board of Trustees, whose responsibility it is to protect insofar as is humanly possible the art objects housed in this institution.

Protective War Measures

After Pearl Harbor was bombed on December 7, 1941, we realized that immediate action had to be taken to safeguard the invaluable collection of paintings, porcelains, manuscripts and books, and other objects housed in the various buildings.

The ceiling of the new gallery was made of glass and had skylights. It was therefore considered the most vulnerable spot and the one to engage our first concern. Professional work was called for in taking care of this situation.

Most of the routine work about the institution ceased soon after that momentous date. Every member of the superintendent's staff who was at all handy with hammer and saw was set busily to work making boxes and crates of various sizes and construction. These were to be used eventually in the packing of special objects for storage, or transportation to more protected inland areas, should the progress of hostilities warrant such action.

All of these cases were carefully numbered when the time came to use them, the contents identified, and an accurate record made by Mr. Block, Curator of the Art Collections. Each case was meticulously designed to fit the individual item to be encased, and they were assembled with screws to avoid the harsh jarring that the necessity of hammering would have caused. The use of screws also facilitated access to the paintings for the periodical inspection that was deemed extremely essential while they were undergoing that period of enclosure in storage. These cases were also cushioned with felt wherever the wooden structure would be in close contact with the painting.

The next step was to build forty-five special containers for the art treasures exhibited in the Arabella Huntington Memorial: these were designated as "A plus" in value and importance. So delicate were some of these items that they required double boxing. The procedure was this: after wrapping each piece in soft cotton, an outer covering of shredded paper was added, and then still another of corrugated cardboard. This was placed in a box surrounded by more soft packing material. At this point in the operation the top was screwed onto the box, the box set into a larger container with about six inches of excelsior cushioning all sides. After the original forty-five cases had been filled, another fifty-seven were built to contain certain specially selected pieces. These were held in reserve until it was deemed a necessary precaution to pack and move them away to safer quarters. Special cases were made also to carry the famous Beauvais tapestries, but were held in reserve for a time. Lastly, three hundred boxes were constructed in which to pack the most valuable part of the priceless collection of rare books and manuscripts.

The packing of the paintings and other pieces of art was left to the discretion of the curators, myself, and a few of the trusted maintenance men, including Paul Kley, George Chaplin, R. F. Drew, and John Gombotz. These men worked hard and long hours in order to prepare most carefully the material for storage and possible transport. The packing of the books was done by the Curator of Rare Books, Robert O. Schad, and his staff, and of the manuscripts by Herbert C. Schulz, Curator of Manuscripts.

Another major operation involved the covering of the skylights in the west wing of the library building, which housed the Arabella Huntington Memorial. Coverings of slabs of re-enforced concrete were considered necessary protection. Precaution was also taken to safeguard the buildings from incendiary bombs. Hand pumps and buckets of sand were located at frequent intervals throughout the buildings, and on all flat roofs pipe lines were installed with hydrants placed every seventy-five feet. Sixteen 50-foot hose lengths were available at strategic points. Close-fitting shutters were installed over all air intakes in the main buildings as provision against a possible enemy poison gas attack. Staff members were organized for day and night duty, furthermore, to guard against air raids. Emergency squads were organized on behalf of the welfare of visitors, should there have occurred a raid during exhibition hours. All in all, it was February 1942 before sufficient precautionary measures were considered to have been taken to protect personnel and treasured goods on the premises.

It was then considered time to plan for the moving of the most valuable books and manuscripts to safer areas. Plans were soon afoot for me to leave for the Rocky Mountain region to examine the storage space available in public and private institutions and warehouses. I was sent on a survey trip, and then on a second trip in May 1942 to deliver personally three cases of books and manuscripts to the First National Bank of Denver. Since this particular consignment of books included the most valuable material in the library, all arrangements were made to transport them under a veil of secrecy. First they were boxed and called for at the library about 5 P.M. on May 4th, by an armored car. Because I was to accompany the goods at every step en route, I was locked in with the boxes until we reached the Union Station in Los Angeles. I delivered them to the express agent, accepted the precious receipt for their care, and remained beside the doors of the Railway Express car, which had been attached to the train, until the latter pulled out on the first lap of its journey. Wherever the train stopped, regardless of the size of the station, between Los Angeles and Denver, I again kept watch over the car that was carrying our priceless cargo.

Arriving in Denver, I was met by an armored car whose guard contingent loaded the boxes into the car and together we delivered them to the First National Bank of Denver. The bank officials sealed the boxes once more and gave me a receipt indicating that they were now custodians of this invaluable collection of material. It was with a sigh of relief that I sent a wire to my wife advising her of the complete success of my trip, and I then headed for my hotel room for the first undisturbed night's rest in some time. A few months after the termination of the war, Mr. Schad traveled to Denver and personally accompanied the same three boxes of books on their return trip to San Marino.

The various emergency measures initiated to safeguard the Huntington Library and Art Gallery, from December 15, 1941, to June 1, 1942, figured precisely 4,227 man-hours of work. These hours were assigned for the most part to members of the superintendent's staff, causing a serious drain on the maintenance personnel. Through all this trying period, the visiting public was accorded access to the exhibitions that could be kept open, and in all ways possible a normal procedure was adhered to.

The handicaps suffered in trying to retain a crew of able personnel for the care of buildings and grounds were immense. This was chiefly because men of high quality were required for the positions of caretakers in the art gallery and for the specialized work entailed throughout the institution. Gardeners and maintenance men had always been needed who were physically fit, but who also appreciated the scope of responsible work in connection with the museum treasures and with the valued plant collections through the vast estate. Such men were no longer available. The majority of the younger men were, of course, inducted into the various branches of the armed services. Older men understandably left our employ to accept more financially attractive offers so freely being made to attract defense plant workers. The few men who were occasionally available were of a type totally unsuited to the defense plant work, because of advanced age or serious physical handicaps. Sometimes wholly inexperienced men applied for work, but they usually seemed unwilling to accept suggestions entailing even a modicum of hard work.

Incredible as it may sound, this situation was even more critical after the Japanese had been interned. Temporary laborers whom we had been obliged to hire left our employ to accept gardening jobs on private estates which paid them from a dollar to a dollar and a half per hour, regardless of their limited abilities. This sudden abnormal rise in wages of common labor was another contributing factor to our inability to maintain the needed personnel. Such an institution as ours simply could not meet such wages. From 1942 to 1946 inclusive we carried on our work here without gardeners: the wonder of it is that we did not lose much more of our horticultural collection than we did.

The Plant Collection

During Mr. Huntington's lifetime, the acquisition of plants to build up our collection proceeded in a most natural manner—by purchase, and by propagation on our own premises. The Department of Agriculture began to send us a few plants occasionally for experimental purposes to test their suitability to California soil, and to the climatic conditions in this part of the country. Then, too, I had always been extremely interested in the growing of rare and exotic plants and was constantly on the alert for them. In the early days, I spent most of my Sundays driving in a horse and buggy to the various Southern California nurseries, looking for the unknown, unusual plant—often found tucked away in a neglected corner of the nursery.

Alfred Roeder, owner of a small nursery on Valley Boulevard, presented me with my first plant gift in 1906: this consisted of a single root each of two giant bamboos, *Bambusa vulgaris,* commonly called Feathery Bamboo, and one held by Mr. Roeder as *Dendrocalamus latiflorus,* but later identified by Dr. F. A. McClure as *Sinocalamus oldhami.* The method of acquiring these was unorthodox but not unusual in those days. I had been admiring the specimens planted along the rear fence of the nursery and said to Roeder that I'd like to purchase some small plants of these two particular species, having in mind to plant them near one of our water gardens. He had none ready for sale, so he gave me a pick and shovel and allowed me to dig up the single roots of each of the two species I had admired. In time these roots developed into huge specimen plants and they are still very much in evidence near the lily ponds.

In 1918 the Department of Agriculture sent us an avocado collection of the Guatemalan variety. In subsequent years from the same source other fruit-bearing trees and ornamental plants were received for experimental purposes. These were increasingly welcome, for after Mr. Huntington's death, the acquisition of new plants through purchasing channels was considerably restricted because of the limitations that a comparably small budget imposed. The Trustees were in sympathy with the plan to increase the plant collection but could go only so far as the budget allowed. In order to augment the collection to a greater extent than might have been possible under those circumstances, I initiated a policy of obtaining new plant material through the process of exchange with other institutions and horticultural establishments, and by outright gifts solicited from interested parties to whom the educational or some other benefit appealed. The greater number of new plants, however, resulted from my personal contacts with nurserymen, horticulturists and owners of, or workers on, private estates or botanic gardens, as well as officials of the plant-distribution section of the Department of Agriculture.

As a matter of detailed record, according to our statistics since 1930, 450 plants have been received from Europe, 150 from Mexico, 100 from Australia, 45 from Africa, 350 from botanic gardens, 1,200 from the Forestry Department, 2,275 from private parties, 5,370 from the Department of Agriculture: a total of 9,940 plants in gifts. This would appear to serve as a testimonial to the contributors who justifiably believed that the Huntington gardens were fast acquiring a world-wide reputation for possessing a valuable and extensive collection of rare and exotic plant specimens.

The year 1940 initiated an occasional practice of the Friends of the Huntington Library to make plant donations. At that time they contributed twenty hardy orchids or cymbidiums, imported from England. The same year another outstanding gift came from Harry J. Butcher of Durban, South Africa, in the form of some rare cycads.

It should be noted here that the loss of plants due to uncommonly unfavorable climatic conditions was negligible over a period of forty-three years. The greatest loss occurred in January 1937, during the all-time record cold spell, which lasted from January 7th to the 11th, and again from January 20th to the 24th. Here are the actual records taken on the night of January 22nd:

6 P.M. 32°	10 P.M. 26°	2 A.M. 21°	6 A.M. 19°
7 P.M. 30°	11 P.M. 25°	3 A.M. 20°	7 A.M. 20°
8 P.M. 28°	12 P.M. 23°	4 A.M. 20°	8 A.M. 20°
9 P.M. 27°	1 A.M. 22°	5 A.M. 19°	

At 10 A.M. that same morning the temperature was still 28° F. in shady sections. During the month of March in 1938 another somewhat disastrous climatic event occurred. A very severe windstorm which lasted three days and three nights uprooted or otherwise damaged a total of 512 trees. Most of the damage, fortunately, was done to acacias and pines which, although considered a great loss, could be replaced fairly readily.

Our plant collection was notably enriched in 1943 through friendly connections with the Southern California Camellia Society. After a series of informal discussions and negotiations with the officials of that society, and with the subsequent permission of the Trustees of the Huntington Library, plans were laid to establish a camellia test garden adjoining and surrounding the Japanese garden. The purpose of the specialized section was to provide opportunity for assembling systematically all known varieties of camellias—a project of educational and scientific value, both to students of this particular genus and to the general public. The nomenclature of existing varieties is at present in a confused state inasmuch as many of the varieties are sold on the market under more than one name. In some cases as many as nine different names have been used for one variety, much to the annoyance of the home gardener or student. At the present writing, about 400 varieties of camellias have been placed in the test garden. An effort is being made to label the plants correctly so that visitors may have the opportunity of viewing and studying them during their flowering season and thus become acquainted with their standard names. If European and Australian varieties can be imported in the future, it is believed that we can increase our collection, in time, to an excess of 1,000 varieties.

Pinetum

About the time plans were being formulated for the camellia test garden, I was looking for a suitable location in the undeveloped area north of the proposed camellia garden where a pinetum could be established. It was my plan to grow all varieties of cone-bearing trees such as pines, cedars, cypresses, and to include unusual genera such as araucarias, agathis, cunninghamias, etc. This project led to correspondence with federal, state and county officials in the forestry departments and resulted in splendid co-operation on their part as they donated numerous seeds and young plants. We feel now that a most satisfactory beginning has been made toward establishing our arboretum, having 1,200 plants of many varieties and exotic types as the beginning of an extensive program which we earnestly hope may be of value from an educational point of view.

Curtailment of Expansion

Between 1939 and 1941, as an economy measure, an area of approximately eight acres planted in 1875 to seedling oranges, a ten-acre persimmon orchard, and five acres of avocados were abandoned. The area vacated by eliminating the seedling orange orchard was replanted in 1943 to a collection of eucalyptus trees, most of which were donated by the Department of Agriculture, 1,000 in all. These were later augmented by donations from the Friends of the Huntington Library.

Plans to establish a hedge test garden to demonstrate the various plants suitable for hedges had to be abandoned for economic reasons; and for similar reasons the planting of a plot of medicinal herbs had to be postponed, although for the latter project a collection of such herbs had been contributed by Mrs. Charles H. Wright of San Marino. Early in 1948 several borders of herbs and a few specimen plantings were made in the wishing-well garden, a setting that lends itself to informal development of an old-fashioned herb garden. This garden was at one time Mrs. Huntington's favorite small garden on the estate; she had it planted to roses and annual borders.

Succession of Trustees

When the deed of trust was executed on August 30, 1919, setting aside the presently used 200 acres for anticipated public use, Mr. Huntington appointed five Trustees: William E. Dunn serving as chairman, supported by George S. Patton; Howard Huntington, Henry E. Huntington's son; Archer M. Huntington, son of Collis P. Huntington; and Dr. George Ellery Hale.

When Mr. Dunn passed away in 1925, Dr. Robert A. Millikan was appointed in his place, while Mr. Patton succeeded Mr. Dunn as chairman. In 1922, Howard Huntington had passed away and Henry M. Robinson accepted the appointment to fill his place. The latter served as vice-chairman under Mr. Patton's leadership, and succeeded him as chairman when Mr. Patton passed away in 1927, at which time Henry S. Pritchett was appointed to fill the new vacancy.

The ranks continued to be cut down by death or resignation: Dr. Pritchett resigned in 1936 and was replaced by the Honorable Herbert Clark Hoover; at Mr. Robinson's death in 1937, Dr. Robert A. Millikan became chairman of the board by election, while Dr. William B. Munro was appointed to fill the vacancy on the board. Dr. Hale passed away in 1938 and in his place Dr. Edwin P. Hubble was appointed. When Archer M. Huntington resigned in 1945, James R. Page accepted the appointment and was elected treasurer. Thus the board continues to function, carrying on the vision of the Founder of this remarkable institution.

Conclusion

It would be in order to mention here the fact that, during the many and sometimes trying years, my own thought and action have always been to fulfill the trust and confidence that Mr. Huntington placed in me to carry out his ideas and wishes pertaining to San Marino Ranch.

Since retiring from active duty, and with the responsibilities resting upon the shoulders of my successor, Ronald B. Townsend, I hope to devote more time to specialized work for which I have heretofore lacked ample opportunity. A few items come to mind still to be accomplished, and yet I feel confident that the over-all picture—"The Dream Place" which Mr. Huntington envisioned and loved so well—has achieved its primary objective: namely, to be enjoyed and to benefit people in all walks of life.

I, for one, am indeed very proud and happy to have had the privilege of playing even a small part in such a worth-while enterprise which has already known success and which promises much more.

Afterword

Since 1948, the following new or improved features have been added to the grounds:

1958–1959. The Shakespeare Garden

1963–1964. The Australian Garden

1964–1965. The Subtropical Garden

1965–1966. The Zen Garden and Bonsai Court

1971–1972. The redesigned Rose Garden

1975–1976. The redesigned Herb Garden

1978–1979. New parking lot and entrance complex

The Jungle Garden

1982–1983. The Virginia Steele Scott Gallery

The new Shakespeare Garden

The Desert Garden Conservatory